D0119371

Measuring Judicial Activism

Measuring Judicial Activism

STEFANIE A. LINDQUIST  FRANK B. CROSS

OXFORD
UNIVERSITY PRESS

OXFORD
UNIVERSITY PRESS

Oxford University Press, Inc., publishes works that further Oxford University's objective of excellence in research, scholarship, and education.

Oxford   New York
Auckland   Cape Town   Dar es Salaam   Hong Kong   Karachi   Kuala Lumpur   Madrid   Melbourne
Mexico City   Nairobi   New Delhi   Shanghai   Taipei   Toronto

With offices in
Argentina   Austria   Brazil   Chile   Czech Republic   France   Greece   Guatemala   Hungary   Italy
Japan   Poland   Portugal   Singapore   South Korea   Switzerland   Thailand   Turkey   Ukraine
Vietnam

Library of Congress Cataloging-in-Publication Data

Lindquist, Stefanie A., 1963-
  Measuring judicial activism / Stefanie A. Lindquist and Frank B. Cross.
    p. cm.
  Includes bibliographical references and index.
  ISBN 978-0-19-537085-0 (hardback : acid-free paper)
1. United States. Supreme Court. 2. Political questions and judicial
power—United States. 3. Judicial review—United States.
I. Cross, Frank B. II. Title.
  KF8742.L56 2009
  347.73'12—dc22
                                                    2008050035

1 2 3 4 5 6 7 8 9

Printed in the United States of America on acid-free paper

Note to Readers
This publication is designed to provide accurate and authoritative information in regard to the subject matter covered. It is based upon sources believed to be accurate and reliable and is intended to be current as of the time it was written. It is sold with the understanding that the publisher is not engaged in rendering legal, accounting, or other professional services. If legal advice or other expert assistance is required, the services of a competent professional person should be sought. Also, to confirm that the information has not been affected or changed by recent developments, traditional legal research techniques should be used, including checking primary sources where appropriate.

(Based on the Declaration of Principles jointly adopted by a Committee of the American Bar Association and a Committee of Publishers and Associations.)

For our mothers. ✳ S.A.L., F.B.C.

Contents

Acknowledgments

WE ARE GRATEFUL TO numerous friends, colleagues, and students for their assistance with this book. First, we would like to thank Dean Larry Sager of the University of Texas School of Law for providing a sabbatical and other resources that enabled us to complete the manuscript. Professor Bernie Black was also extremely generous with funding for research assistants. We also wish to thank Dean Edward Rubin of the Vanderbilt University School of Law for providing Lindquist with summer funding for purposes of completing the data collection process.

We have also benefited from the assistance of many graduate, undergraduate, and law students who worked hard to help us gather and refine data or who proofed or cite-checked our sources: Jennifer Selin, Jessica Hart, Jonathan Patton, Marine Ghulyan, Fernanda Boidi, Matthew E. Simpson, Muralidharan Jagannathan, Helena Coronado-Salazar, Jenna Lukasik, Tyler Bexley, and John Hudak. We are also indebted to Harold Spaeth and Sara Benesh for compiling the remarkable United States Supreme Court Judicial Database for public use and to Kirk Randazzo for maintaining the Web site that makes the data so easy to obtain. Thanks also go to Paul Collins and Joe Smith for some programming assistance. Lindquist would also like to thank Jim Morris for his moral support and remarkable proofreading abilities, Rorie Spill Solberg and Joe Smith for their great co-authorship on earlier related projects, and Lori Ringhand for her willingness to review parts of the manuscript and offer suggestions. We would also like to thank our dedicated and professional editors at OUP, including Chris Collins, Isel Pizarro, Jaimee Biggins and Liz Kaplan.

List of Figures and Tables

ONE

The Political and Academic Debate Over Judicial Activism

"JUDICIAL ACTIVISM" IS A LOADED TERM, fraught with multiple meanings and politicized connotations. As a result, activism, like beauty, is often in the eye of the beholder (Sherry 2007, 1065). Nevertheless, concerns over judicial activism have existed since the founding of the United States. For the most part, those who decry activist decisions focus on the judiciary's usurpation of political power from the elected branches, especially when judges render those decisions in accordance with their own policy preferences. As Alexander Hamilton expressed it in *The Federalist 78*, "[t]he Courts must declare the sense of the law; and if they should be disposed to exercise will instead of judgment, the consequences would equally be the substitution of their pleasure for that of the legislative body" (Hamilton 1788, 440).

Especially in the latter part of the twentieth century, criticisms of judicial activism have become woven into the warp and woof of American politics. In this chapter, we trace the political and intellectual history of the term. The theoretical analysis of activism, discussed in the latter part of this chapter, lays the foundation for our efforts in Chapter 2 to define the term more systematically for purposes of empirical measurement.

✹ A. Early Conceptions of Activism

The origin of the term "judicial activism" may be traced to Arthur Schlesinger. In a 1947 article for *Fortune* magazine, he profiled the justices of the Supreme Court, dividing them into "activists" (Justices Black, Douglas, Murphy, and Rutledge) and "champions of judicial restraint" (Justices Frankfurter, Jackson, and Burton). As he described it, activist judges were those most willing to employ judicial power "for their own conception of the social good," while restraintist judges focused more on "expanding the range of allowable judgment for legislatures" (Schlesinger 1947, 201). Consistent with this perspective, judicial activism has become synonymous with judicial decision making that inappropriately crowds out the policy-making prerogatives of the elected branches.

Although the term is attributed to Schlesinger, the theoretical underpinnings to the idea of judicial activism are far more historic. Concerns about activist judging arose in connection with the framing of the Constitution, with Hamilton's response in *Federalist 78* offering a palliative to those who were apprehensive about judicial power. Yet despite Hamilton's assurances that the judiciary was "the least dangerous branch" (Hamilton, 1788, 437), concerns persisted. Soon after the founding, Jeffersonian Republicans complained that the Federalist judiciary was undermining congressional prerogatives (Peabody 2007, 190). In 1861, Abraham Lincoln argued in his first inaugural address that if political issues were resolved by the judiciary, "the people will have ceased to be their own rulers" (Lincoln 1861).

At the turn of the twentieth century, charges of inappropriate policy making were leveled at the Supreme Court's conservative decisions invalidating economic regulations, especially its 1905 decision in *Lochner v. New York*[1] which overturned a New York law limiting the number of hours bakers could work (Gillman 1993). *Lochner* set the stage for the Court's invalidation of New Deal legislation and is often presented as an archetypal example of judicial activism, reflecting the Court's refusal to defer to the legislature on matters of economic regulation (Powers and Rothman 2002, 21). As a result of decisions like *Lochner*, Franklin Delano Roosevelt famously proposed "packing" the Supreme Court with justices sympathetic to his policies.[2]

Although these early critics of judicial power did not use the term "judicial activism," they clearly invoked it in principle, usually in criticism of the Court. As Arthur Selwyn Miller observed, "[f]rom time to time since 1803, the Supreme Court has been harshly criticized for being too activist, not always, however, for the same reasons or by the same groups" (A. S. Miller 1982, 6). Yet not all commentators have condemned judicial activism. In his fine review of the concept, Keenan D. Kmiec suggested that "[i]n its early days, the term 'judicial activist' sometimes had a positive connotation, much more akin to 'civil rights activist' than 'judge misusing authority'" (Kmiec 2004, 1451).

---

1. 198 U.S. 45 (1905).

2. Indeed, Justice Ruth Bader Ginsburg has labeled the *Lochner*-era Court the most activist in United States history (Kramer 2007, 42).

Certainly *Brown v. Board of Education*,[3] which terminated judicial support for segregated education, is widely viewed as an activist decision, yet it has achieved iconic status as a symbol of social justice (Sowell 2004, Egelko 2004). Indeed, the *Brown* decision, along with other Warren Court opinions promoting an expansive view of social and political rights, initiated the current debate over judicial activism.

≋ B. The Warren Court

In both popular and academic discourse, the Warren Court has become the poster child for judicial activism. This association is made clear in a *Dictionary of Politics* published in 1992, which defines judicial activism as "[t]he practice of some Justices of the U.S. Supreme Court (e.g., Chief Justice Earl Warren 1953–1969; Associate Justices Hugo Black, 1937–1971; William O. Douglas, 1939–1975; and William J. Brennan, 1956–) to disregard established judicial precedents or even some principles of law (favoring statutory rather than constitutional law) in order to protect and to broaden individual rights as political, economic, and social conditions may require" (Raymond 1992, 256).

Without question, the Warren Court was staffed by a number of justices willing to wield the Court's power to promote social change. Soon after Earl Warren was sworn in as chief justice, the Court began to render dramatic rulings protecting individual rights and eliminating segregation. These rulings quickly provoked a backlash from Southerners. According to the Southern Manifesto signed by nearly every legislator from the Deep South, *Brown* was a "clear abuse of judicial power" reflecting a "trend in the Federal judiciary undertaking to legislate" (U.S. Senate 1956, 102, pt. 2:4515–16). The attack grew in strength in the late 1950s, as the Court issued a series of decisions protecting the civil liberties of Communists. When the Court banned compulsory prayer in schools, calls for the justices' impeachment grew. Additional decisions supporting the rights of criminal defendants were likewise regarded as inappropriate activism. The common claim was that "liberal, activist constitutionalism" destroyed majority rights (Howard and Segal 2004, 132).

---

3. 347 U.S. 483 (1954).

Much of the animosity centered on the chief justice himself. Earl Warren was said to be the "paradigm of the result-oriented judge" who used his judicial authority to promote his own personal view of social justice (Belknap 2005, 311). As one source has reported, Warren reputedly asked attorneys making legal arguments, "Yes, Counsel, but is it fair?" (Kalman 1996, 46). Other Warren Court justices exhibited behavior that also appeared result-oriented, as illustrated by Justice Fortas's practice of writing opinions without citation and asking his clerks to "decorate" them with necessary legal support (Kalman 1996, 46). Criticism of this result-oriented activism emerged not only from popular sources, but also from prominent legal experts such as Alexander Bickel, Learned Hand, Philip Kurland, and Herbert Wechsler. In the pages of the *Harvard Law Review*, Henry Hart declared that the Warren Court in one decision "gave gratuitous aid and comfort to the most extreme of its critics who say that it twists facts and words at its pleasure in order to reach the results it wants to reach" (Hart 1959, 122).

The extent to which the Warren Court was willing to shape legal rights in accordance with the justices' own visions of public morality is well-illustrated by its decision in *Griswold v. Connecticut*,[4] regarded generally as an activist recognition of privacy rights. In his majority opinion, Justice Douglas opined that the Court does not "sit as a super-legislature to determine the wisdom, need, and propriety of laws that touch economic problems, business affairs, or social conditions."[5] Yet his opinion arguably did exactly that, relying on the penumbra implied by six different provisions of the Bill of Rights. Because the decision rested on "penumbras" rather than on any specific textual support for privacy rights, the decision in *Griswold* became associated with "judicial lawlessness" (e.g., Bork 1990).

Although many commentators identify activism with the Warren Court, the scope of the Warren Court's activism has been debated—at least in its impact. In his highly praised book *The Hollow Hope: Can Courts Bring About Social Change* (1991), Gerald Rosenberg argues persuasively that even the Warren Court's most notably activist decisions had little impact alone on the social problems they addressed. Moreover, the Warren Court responded meekly to some of the most heavily contested political issues of the day. It ducked the Vietnam War controversy and gave only the very slightest of nods to income redistribution, providing some due process rights to welfare

---

4. 381 U.S. 479 (1965).

5. *Id.* at 482.

recipients but hardly achieving a welfare rights revolution. Instead, the Court was most involved in issues of individual rights, including the rights of criminal defendants and minorities. Many of the most significant of these decisions remain intact, suggesting that, despite the frequent criticism, efforts to undermine the Court's standing "brought no literal change or damage to the Court or its rulings" (Wicker 2002, 6). The public apparently respects or has acquiesced in many of the Warren Court's decisions (Beth 1961, 22). Notably, one seldom hears criticism today of what are, arguably, among the Warren Court's most activist decisions, including *Brown*, *Gideon v. Wainwright*[6] (granting indigents the right to legal counsel in criminal cases), or *Reynolds v. Sims*[7] (requiring equal population distribution among state legislative districts).

The continued relevance of the Warren Court's rulings and their relative immunity to change over time may stem in part from the fact that most of that Court's decisions invalidated local or state laws or actions rather than those supported by a national majority. One close analysis of the Court found that its activism was focused almost entirely on laws enacted by Southern states (such as segregation), those prompted by pre-Vatican II Catholicism, and a few local law enforcers (Powe 2000, 492–494). Thus the Warren Court's activism must be viewed carefully in light of the scope of its decisions.

〽 C. Judicial Activism beyond the Warren Court

1. The Burger Court

Although sworn in to the presidency by Chief Justice Warren himself, Richard Nixon had pledged during his campaign to appoint justices who would not read their own preferences into the ambiguous clauses of the Constitution. Three years after his inauguration, Nixon appointed four new justices to the Supreme Court, including new Chief Justice Warren Burger. Nixon's objective in appointing these more conservative justices was to reorient the Court's policies away from the liberal outcomes championed by Earl Warren and his brethren. As a result, Court observers anticipated that the Burger Court would retrench the Warren Court precedents. Yet, in part because Nixon's appointees did not constitute a majority on the Court, the Burger Court did not reverse the Warren Court's most salient decisions (Wasby 1976).

---

6. 372 U.S. 335 (1963).

7. 377 U.S. 533 (1964).

The major pillars of the Warren Court's jurisprudence, including those involving civil rights, defendants' rights, and reapportionment, remained largely unaffected by the Burger Court (Blasi 1986). Indeed, although Nixon's "Southern Strategy" was aimed at winning votes from disaffected white voters in the South, the Burger Court did little to mollify that constituency by limiting *Brown v. Board of Education*. Instead, shortly after Burger's appointment as chief justice, the Court reaffirmed and continued to enforce *Brown's* mandate that southern schools desegregate "with all deliberate speed." Thereafter the Burger Court provided limited support for the use of busing as a tool to integrate school children. Perhaps most remarkably, it was the Burger Court that issued *Roe v. Wade*.[8] Based as it is on the right to privacy announced in *Griswold, Roe* remains for many the prominent example of undue judicial activism. Similarly, the Burger Court continued to uphold a careful separation between church and state. In an important First Amendment case, *Lemon v. Kurtzman*,[9] for example, the Burger Court struck down a Pennsylvania law allowing state funds to be used to support religious educational institutions. Although some commentators have questioned its continued vitality (e.g., Kahle 2005), the *Lemon* test for determining the constitutionality of church-state relations nevertheless remains among the Court's most influential First Amendment doctrines.

Thus the Burger Court largely failed to "undo" the Warren Court's most salient precedents. And for some, the Burger Court continued to represent the worst of an activist judiciary, particularly in the light of decisions such as *Roe v. Wade*. For example, conservative judge J. Harvie Wilkinson III has referred to "the excessive activism of the Warren and Burger Courts" (Wilkinson 2002, 1383), while others have claimed that Warren Court activism "lived on" in the "superactivism" of the Burger Court (Belknap 2005, 312; Schick 1984, 49). As a result, conservatives continued to attack "government by the judiciary" through the Burger years (Keck 2004, 109).

2. The Rehnquist Court

Like Richard Nixon before him, Ronald Reagan entered office on a platform that included a strong opposition to judicial activism, proclaiming that he

---

8. 410 U.S. 113 (1973).

9. 403 U.S. 602 (1971).

would appoint only judges "who understand the danger of short-circuiting the electoral process and disenfranchising the people through judicial activism" (Reagan 1985). More particularly, Reagan complained of judicial leniency toward criminals that was "the result of another liberal phenomenon: judicial activism; judges who thought it was their right to make the law, not just interpret it; judges who fashioned new rules that were a catastrophe for law abiding citizens, new rules that made it harder to convict even the most hardened and obvious criminals" (Reagan 1987). Reagan favored judges who would draw back such leniency.

When Warren Burger retired in 1986, Ronald Reagan appointed William Rehnquist to the position of chief justice. At that time, Rehnquist represented the far right anchor on the Court. With Rehnquist's elevation, and the appointment of Justice Antonin Scalia in the same year, Reagan was able to move the Supreme Court's ideological orientation to the right. Although Reagan's other appointees O'Connor and Kennedy were more moderately conservative than Rehnquist and Scalia, they nevertheless shifted the center of the Court to the right as well. Many observers anticipated that this change would result in a new era of judicial restraint on the Court. Yet commentators are somewhat divided over whether the Rehnquist Court fulfilled this promise.

First, although the Rehnquist Court was conservative on many issues, it nevertheless rendered some liberal rulings (largely supported by the Rehnquist Court's liberal bloc) that drew criticism from conservatives charging activism. The Court's decision in *Lawrence v. Texas*,[10] striking the Texas sodomy statute, has been condemned by conservatives as the worst form of judicial activism. In his *Lawrence* dissent, Justice Scalia accused the majority of "taking sides in the culture war" over homosexuality and of abandoning its rightful role to "assur[e], as neutral observer, that the democratic rules of engagement are observed."[11] Ken Connor of the conservative Family Research Council reviled the decision as "classic judicial activism arrogance" (quoted in N. A. Lewis 2003, A19). Similarly, conservative critics have condemned the Court's decisions in *Hamdi v. Rumsfeld*[12] and *Rasul v. Bush*,[13] which provided some constitutional protections to enemy combatants in the Bush

---

10. 539 U.S. 558 (2003)

11. *Id.* at 602 (Scalia, J., dissenting).

12. 542 U.S. 507 (2004).

13. 542 U.S. 466 (2004).

Administration's so-called "War on Terror." These latter two decisions challenged the authority of the executive branch in relation to its policy in that area.

The Rehnquist Court has not been criticized solely for its more liberal activist rulings, however. With the ascent of a conservative Supreme Court, accusations that conservatives are the "real judicial activists" have become frequent (Kerr 2003, 31), with some observers even claiming that the Rehnquist Court is the most activist in history (e.g., Keck 2004). According to Cass Sunstein, for example, the Rehnquist Court shepherded in "a remarkable period of right-wing judicial activism" (Sunstein 2001, A23). Erwin Chemerinsky has also criticized conservative judges for aggressively pursuing an agenda of conservative judicial activism (Chemerinsky 2000, B11), while Jack Balkin and Sandy Levinson have argued that the Warren Court's "judicial activism has been replaced with one much harsher and more conservative" (Balkin and Levinson 2001, 1092).

Many of these criticisms focus on the Rehnquist Court's willingness to invalidate congressional enactments under the Commerce Clause or the Tenth and Eleventh Amendments, often in the service of federalism principles.[14] Under these precedents, Congress's power is curtailed in favor of state prerogatives.[15] Conservative justices have also been charged with what has been called "partisan judicial activism," describing those decisions rendered to benefit one political party or appointing president (W. P. Marshall 2002, 1245). According to critics, cases involving partisan activism include the ruling in *Clinton v. Jones*,[16] allowing the continued pursuit of sexual harassment claims against President Clinton, and *Department of Commerce v. United States House of Representatives*,[17] siding with the Republicans on the use of the census in determining electoral districts. The decision in

---

14. As Lori Ringhand points out, however, conservative justices on the Rehnquist Court also invalidated a number of congressional enactments on First Amendment grounds as well (Ringhand 2007).

15. For a discussion of the Rehnquist Court's federalism jurisprudence in the context of judicial review, see Dow, Jeu, and Coveny (2008). Although clearly counter-majoritarian to the extent federal laws reflect the preferences of a national majority, this form of judicial activism has defenders. Judge J. Harvie Wilkinson, for example, conceded that the federalism jurisprudence had become "judicial activism," but claimed that it was a "constructive" sort of activism. *Brzonkala v. Va. Polytechnic Inst. & State Univ.*, 169 F.3d 820, 892–893 (4th Cir. 1999) (Wilkinson, C.J., concurring).

16. 520 U.S. 681 (1997).

17. 525 U.S. 316 (1999).

Bush v. Gore,[18] which effectively resulted in the selection of the president in a close election, was surely the most pronounced example of the Rehnquist Court's so-called partisan activism.

Nevertheless, liberal charges of conservative activism have produced no great concessions from the right. Conservatives still loudly protest an activist liberal judiciary and point to liberal outcomes reached by the Rehnquist Court. In 2004, Attorney General John Ashcroft lamented that "intrusive judicial oversight" could "put at risk the very security of our nation in a time of war" (quoted in Seper 2004). And conservatives continued to find fault with a "virulent resurgence of new activist behavior on the Supreme Court fueled by the votes and influence of President Clinton's two Supreme Court appointees [Ginsburg and Breyer]" (Calabresi 2004, 578–579).

That the Rehnquist Court is attacked from critics of all political persuasions illustrates well how charges of activism often depend on whose ideological ox is being gored. Labeling a court or decision "activist" suggests that the justices have somehow overstepped their institutional boundaries, but the label is usually affixed to decisions based on the substantive policy outcomes they achieve. Although the Warren Court is often associated most closely with activism, the Burger and Rehnquist Courts have also been criticized for activist decision making, suggesting that activism is not solely the province of a liberal court. Indeed, the criticism shows no sign of abatement: recently appointed Chief Justice John Roberts has already been labeled a "raging judicial activist" (A. Cohen 2006, 11).

The foregoing discussion provided a brief history of activism, particularly as it has been associated with the Warren, Burger, and Rehnquist Courts. We now turn to an evaluation of activism in public discourse. How does the public view judicial activism, and what role has the press played in shaping the public debate over activism? How has the term been used as a rhetorical tool by political elites?

D. Judicial Activism in the Public Forum

1. Public and Elite Opinion

At least one observer has suggested that few legal issues "have agitated the American public as much as the controversy over so-called 'judicial activism'"

---

18. 531 U.S. 98 (2000).

(Sandefur 2004, 2). According to a 2005 survey by the American Bar Association, 56% of Americans strongly or somewhat believed that judicial activism was a contemporary "crisis," while 46% strongly or somewhat agreed with the opinion that judges were "arrogant, out-of-control and unaccountable" (Neil 2005). A Gallup poll conducted in 2005 found that only 2% of Americans believe that federal judges do not allow their political views to influence their decisions.[19]

The public's perception of judicial activism has the potential to affect confidence in the courts. In a study of public attitudes toward the Supreme Court between 1966 and 1984, for example, Gregory Caldeira found a negative correlation between judicial activism, as measured by the number of instances in which the Court invalidated federal legislation, and the percentage of yearly survey respondents who expressed "great confidence" in the Supreme Court (Caldeira 1986). While a later study of the same phenomena did not confirm this finding, it did show that public support for the Court is largely dependent on the extent to which the Court's decisions diverge from the policy preferences of the mass public (Durr, Martin, and Wolbrecht 2000).

Media exposure to the issue of judicial activism may also elevate levels of public concern over the issue. In his study of Roosevelt's Court-packing plan launched in response to the Court's conservative activism in relation to New Deal legislation, Caldeira found that the tenor of media attention to the story shaped public attitudes toward the president's plan to curtail the Court's conservative cast (Caldeira 1987). It would not be surprising, therefore, for negative media treatments of judicial activism to influence public attitudes on the matter. Indeed, judicial activism on the Supreme Court has often been prominently discussed on the editorial pages of leading newspapers over time. On the conservative editorial pages of the *Wall Street Journal*, for example, the Warren Court era was characterized as involving "unapologetic judicial activism based more on good intentions than the law" (M. Miller 1997, A16). The *Journal's* criticism has not been limited to the Warren Court, however. In 1984, the editorial page attacked the Burger Court for producing activist decisions rivaling those of the Warren Court (Wermiel 1984). In 1997, the *Journal* further declared that the Court's "judicial activism has reached the outer limits of what this society is willing to tolerate" (M. Miller 1997, A16). Yet as the Court became more conservative, a 2007

---

19. CNN/USA Today/Gallup Poll (April 1–2, 2005). PollingReport.com, http://www.pollingreport.com/court2.htm (accessed June 2008).

Wall Street Journal editorial gave a "cheer for judicial activism," arguing that such activism promoted liberty and the rule of law (Bolick 2007, A15).

The more liberal editorial page of the *New York Times* has also commented occasionally on judicial activism. In 1982, Professor Lloyd Weinreb published an editorial defending activism as a necessary response to the other branches' "mean-spirited disregard" for the disadvantaged (Weinreb 1982, A27). Five years later, Anthony Lewis proffered a similar defense of activism as necessary to protect constitutional rights (A. Lewis 1987, A31). And by 1988, the *Times* had begun to criticize what it viewed as a new conservative activism on the Court. In that year, the editorial page lamented the new judicial activism, "Reagan-Style," in relation to a ruling granting government contractors broad protections from products liability claims (*New York Times* 1988, A26). In response to a series of Supreme Court decisions in its 1998 term invaliding federal protections for persons with disabilities and for state employees, the *Times* editorial page complained that the conservative bloc on the Court, who were "supposedly opposed to judicial activism," had been whittling away at federal Congressional power since 1996 and undermining critical Court precedents (*New York Times* 1999, A26). In this vein, a 2005 *Times* editorial written by two professors counted votes and found that it was the Court's conservative justices who were most likely to favor constitutional invalidation of federal statutes (Gewirtz and Golder 2005). Nicholas Kristof cited this study to argue that judicial activism should be avoided on the right and the left (Kristof 2005). In 2007, the *Times* editorial page further declaimed conservative "judicial activism" and its "dishonesty" (A. Cohen 2007, A16). Similarly, E.J. Dionne has declared that Bush appointees Roberts and Alito are "activist conservatives intent on leading a judicial counterrevolution" (Dionne 2007).

To gauge the level of media attention to judicial activism in recent years, we generated a simple measure of the frequency of references to "judicial activism" in the *New York Times*, *Wall Street Journal*, *Los Angeles Times*, *Washington Post*, and *Chicago Tribune*, from 1985 to the present. Figure 1 displays the annual combined frequency with which activism was mentioned in these papers, whether those references were negative, positive, or neutral.

For most of this period, the number of references to activism fluctuated from the 20s to nearly 100, with intermittent spikes. The amount of press coverage peaked around the beginning of the Rehnquist Court and the appointment of Justice Scalia in 1986, followed by the failed attempt to nominate Robert Bork to the Court. The dramatic spike in 2005 is associated with the nomination of John Roberts as chief justice, and far surpassed the level of

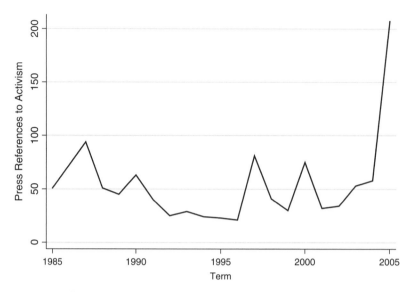

FIGURE 1 References to Judicial Activism in Major Newspapers, 1985–2005

attention in connection with prior nominations. Thus, even though judicial activism is often associated with the Warren Court era, it continues to be a matter of major public concern today.

Because criticisms of judicial activism appear to resonate with the public, activism obviously ranks high on politicians' agenda as well. Of course, the direction of causality here is unclear: elite opinion may drive mass opinion on this issue rather than other way around (B. Jones 1994, 122). Indeed, to the extent activist decisions displace choices made by elected officials, they frustrate the ability of politicians to achieve their desired policy objectives. Candidates may therefore appeal to their constituencies by promising to favor only the appointment of "strict constructionist" judges. As Judge William Wayne Justice observed:

> For the past 20 years, every United States Supreme Court nominee has come with a presidential warranty that he or she will be a jurist who interprets the law rather than makes it. It has become commonplace for political office-seekers and officeholders of all ideological stripes to make 'judicial activism' the target of much demagogic bluster (Wayne 1997, 302).

Thus, whether or not the invocation of activism often seems to constitute "mindless incantation," it is apparently politically useful rhetoric. For that reason, discussion of judicial activism has become important to political discourse (Chemerinsky 2002, 2020).

Public interest in judicial activism has either caused or been fueled in part by books published in the popular press that address the issue. The conservative critique of judicial activism is well-illustrated by Mark Levin's recent book *Men in Black*. In this best-selling book, Levin first takes aim at historical precedents, including *Dred Scott v. Sanford*[20] (1856) (determining whether a slave could claim U.S. citizenry), and *Plessy v. Ferguson*[21] (1896) (upholding the doctrine of separate but equal accommodations for black railroad patrons). Levin claims that, in *Dred Scott*, Chief Justice Roger Taney "imposed his own view [of the law] on the nation," while Levin argues that, in *Plessy*, "an activist Supreme Court upheld a state law that mandated segregation" (Levin 2005, 15–16). With respect to more recent decisions, Levin finds judicial activism in many decisions involving the development of privacy law, the recognition of gay rights, affirmative action, limits on detention of enemy combatants, and broad interpretations of the Commerce Clause. The list has an obvious ideological hue, of course. Levin praises decisions invalidating statutes under the Commerce Clause that limit federal authority but generally criticizes decisions invalidating statutes under other constitutional provisions that yield more liberal results. Thus Levin's critique is essentially a complaint about decisions with which he disagrees, with no neutral principle to define judicial activism other than his personal vision of the Constitution.[22]

Other recent books that address the issue of judicial activism include *The Dirty Dozen: How Twelve Supreme Court Cases Radically Expanded Government and Eroded Freedom* (2008) by Cato Institute scholars Robert A. Levy and William Mellor; *Judicial Tyranny: The New Kings of America* (2005), edited by Mark Sutherland; and *The Myth of the Imperial Judiciary: Why the Right is Wrong About the Courts* (2003) by Mark Kozlowski (and a forward by Anthony Lewis). These popular press books reflect the thrust and parry of the conservative critique and liberal response to charges of judicial activism. That *Men in Black*, in particular, became a *New York Times* bestseller—"flying

---

20. 60 U.S. 393 (1856).

21. 163 U.S. 537 (1896).

22. As an example of this muddled perspective, *Plessy* is viewed as activist because it "forced a private industry . . . to separate individuals on account of race" (Levin 2005, 16). One could make an equally facile argument, however, that *Plessy* was an exercise in judicial restraint because it *upheld* a product of the legislative process.

off the shelves" as one newspaper story put it (Lane 2005, A6)—indicates the degree to which the issue of judicial activism resonates with the public.

2. Confirmation Hearings

Nominations of potential Supreme Court justices provide politicians with the opportunity to highlight their position on judicial activism. Since the confirmation process is the most significant tool by which the Senate may directly control the Court, it is no surprise that Senators concerned about judicial activism attempt to use confirmation hearings to weed out nominees likely to be activist in their orientation—or at least for the senators to publicize their opposition to the practice. In this connection, the modern political controversy over judicial activism became particularly pronounced when President Johnson nominated Abe Fortas for the position of chief justice. Senators questioned Fortas aggressively about liberal activism on the Warren Court; Fortas was even charged with coddling rapists and pornographers (Keck 2004, 107). Although his nomination was ultimately denied on other grounds, the Senate's decision was plainly colored by his association with the perceived liberal activism of the Warren Court.

Yet at least one other nominee has failed to be confirmed because of concerns over conservative activism. At the time Ronald Reagan nominated Robert Bork to the seat vacated by Lewis Powell, rhetorical condemnations of judicial activism had reached a feverish pitch, spurred by Attorney General Edwin Meese's campaign to recruit judicial nominees who shared his commitment to "pure constitutional originalism" (Yalof 1999, 142–143). Speaking in favor of the Bork nomination, Senator Robert Dole argued that the "American people have felt the sting of judicial activism," which had tilted the scales "toward the criminal" and become an approach for denying the people "a say on issues like the death penalty and restrictions on pornography" (U.S. Senate 1987a, 14985). During the same nomination debate, Senator William Roth likened judicial activism to tyranny (U.S. Senate 1987, 14767). Although Ronald Reagan nominated Robert Bork in 1987 because he embraced a method of constitutional interpretation (original intent) that allegedly constrains judicial discretion, liberal critics were concerned that Bork was in fact likely to engage in a conservative form of activism. In particular, they were apprehensive that Bork would retrench Supreme Court precedents protecting civil rights and liberties, especially of minorities and women. As Edward Kennedy stated on the floor of the Senate:

Robert Bork's America is a land in which women would be forced into back alley abortions, blacks would sit at segregated lunch counters, rogue policemen would break down citizen's doors in midnight raids, school children could not be taught about evolution, writers and artists could be censured at the whim of government (quoted in Abraham 1992, 357).

This quotation highlights the differences in perspectives regarding the consequences of competing constitutional visions that shaped the debate over the Bork nomination. Similar objections from influential senators, in combination with massive interest group involvement and Reagan's lame duck status, brought the Bork nomination to defeat.

Following the failed Bork nomination, in recent history some—but not all—Supreme Court nominees have undergone extensive questioning on the issue of judicial activism. In the hearings confirming William Rehnquist as associate justice, the nominee received only brief questioning from Senator Hart regarding Rehnquist's judicial philosophy in relationship to judicial conservatism and restraint. At the time of his nomination to be chief justice in 1986, Rehnquist engaged in a somewhat more extensive discussion of the concept with Senator James Broyhill. In the same year, Justice Scalia was asked only a few questions on "activism" in his confirmation hearings. One was a friendly offering from Senator Oren Hatch and another was from Senator Charles Mathias, who simply sought Scalia's disapproval of an activist judiciary. Similarly, Anthony Kennedy received only a general and sympathetic question on the issue from Senator Chuck Grassley, to which Kennedy could disclaim any intention to engage in activist decision making.

President George H. W. Bush's appointees received somewhat more comprehensive questions on the topic. Senator Dennis DeConcini questioned David Souter on activism in the context of criminal procedure, with a particular focus on the *Miranda* warnings and the death penalty, while Senators Grassley and Strom Thurmond pointedly asked Souter how he defined activism and whether it was ever appropriate. In his response, then-Judge Souter described activism as "a sense of the judge as embodying pure personal policy preferences and value choices, however sincerely they may be felt, as opposed to embodying values which are found and based upon some kind of an objective source of meaning . . . that simply does not force the court into, in effect, giving free rein to its own predilections" (U.S. Senate 1990, 204–205). Much of the discussion of activism during Justice Souter's confirmation hearing then centered on whether it is appropriate for the judiciary to fill "policy vacuums" when the legislature and executive have chosen not to act. A year later during his contentious confirmation hearings, Clarence Thomas was asked by Senator Grassley whether he considered judicial activism legitimate, and he assured the Judiciary Committee that he did not. Thomas did receive one challenging question from Senator Howell Heflin about whether his belief in natural law would likely lead to an activist approach to constitutional interpretation. Further, he was questioned on his view of *Roe v. Wade*, which could be considered an exploration of judicial activism. In terms of questions related to activism, the Thomas confirmation hearings witnessed a distinct increase of concern.

One might expect Democratic appointees to receive more questioning on the topic from Republican senators, and Ruth Bader Ginsburg saw a relatively high level of discussion of judicial activism in her hearing. Senator Thurmond asked Ginsburg about activism in the form of judicial orders imposing taxes. Her questionnaire from the Judiciary Committee also inquired about her views on judicial activism and she was sympathetically questioned by Senator DeConcini about her response. She also received limited questioning from Senators Arlen Specter and Carol Mosely-Braun on the issue. Senator Hatch did question her more directly about the topic but only in the context of the relatively settled controversy over *Dred Scott* and *Lochner*. Stephen Breyer also responded to a questionnaire on the topic and received questions from Senators Hatch and Alan Simpson on the issue of activism, but neither was especially challenging and the number of mentions of judicial activism was well below that of the Ginsburg or Thomas hearings.

The Judiciary Committee's concern for judicial activism—at least as reflected in its questioning of the nominees discussed above—seemed to persist following the retirement of Chief Justice Rehnquist. At his 2005 confirmation hearings, John Roberts received friendly questions about judicial activism from Republican Senators Jeff Sessions, Tom Coburn and Hatch, who were interested in communicating their disapproval of the practice. From the liberal perspective, Senator Charles Schumer questioned Roberts about a memo he wrote while working in the U.S. Attorney General's office regarding whether Brennan and Marshall were activist justices. Most notably, Roberts was subjected to some pointed questioning by Senator Arlen Specter about the Court's recent decisions invalidating federal enactments. Complaining about the Court's creation of a test to evaluate whether Congress had overstepped its institutional prerogatives, Specter declared, "I'm talking about the essence of a man-, woman-made test in the Supreme Court which has no grounding in the Constitution, no grounding in the *Federalist Papers*, no grounding in the history of the country. It comes out of thin air" (U.S. Senate 2005b, 302). Roberts largely demurred to Specter's assault on activist decisions striking federal laws (*see* Greenhouse 2005). In his responses to the Judiciary Committee questionnaire, Roberts committed himself to a position of judicial restraint, asserting that a judge does "not have a commission to solve society's problems" (U.S. Senate 2005b, 163). He further remarked on the importance of modesty and humility in the judicial role.

In the succeeding year, this trend continued with the nomination of Samuel Alito. During those confirmation hearings, Senators Schumer and Herb Kohl challenged conservative judicial activism in relation to the Court's refusal to defer to Congress by invalidating federal enactments. Senators Grassley, Sessions, Sam Brownback, and Jon Kyl also pursued concerns about judicial activism, but from a more conservative perspective.

Confirmation hearings thus provide a highly public forum in which politicians can stake their claim to a restraintist position or advertise their support for existing Court doctrines that are vulnerable to invalidation by the nominee. In relation to activism, then, senators have generally fallen into one of the categories described by Watson and Stookey (1988): evaluator, educator, validator, and partisan. As described above, some senators seek to evaluate the candidate's adherence to principles of restraint, some to educate their constituencies on their position regarding activism, some to validate their belief about the nominee's position on the issue, and some to attack the nominee in pursuance of partisan politics. Regardless of their role, however, individual members of the Senate Judiciary Committee clearly view judicial activism as an important and salient topic for consideration at confirmation hearings.

3. Party Platforms and Political Rhetoric

While it is sometimes suggested that the courts are not a significant feature of political campaigns, politicians have used the issue of judicial activism to promote their candidacies. Although not a politician herself, Phyllis Schlafly nonetheless declared judicial activism to be the "biggest 2002 election issue (Schlafly 2002)."[23] During his 2003 reelection campaign President George W. Bush

---

23. Lamenting a series of Supreme Court decisions involving school prayer, evolution, and other topics, Schlafly complained: "Out went the Ten Commandments, in came condoms. Out went the Cross and pictures of Christ, in came drawings of apes pretending to walk like humans. Out went Adam and Eve, in came *Heather Has Two Mommies*. Out went Easter, in came Earth Day. Out went teachings against homosexuality, in came teachings in favor of homosexuality" (Schlafly 2002).

declared that "I'm a person who believes in judicial restraint, as opposed to judicial activism that takes the place of the legislative branch" (Bush 2003). Candidate Bush further opined that the "excessive judicial activism of the 60's and 70's is the reason Americans turned against that kind of liberalism in the 80's" (quoted in Hoffman 1998, A1). In announcing nominations to the federal judiciary during his first term as president, Bush declared that each of his judicial appointees "will be a person who clearly understands the role of a judge is to interpret the law, not to legislate from the bench" (Bush 2001). In a later State of the Union address, he reiterated that "judges must be servants of the law, and not legislate from the bench" (Bush 2006).

Evidence of the political role of judicial activism might also be found in party platforms. In every platform since 1968, the Republican Party has engaged in some degree of criticism of the federal judiciary, but most did not explicitly refer to judicial activism (Engel 2007). In 1996, however, the Republican platform lamented that the Constitution "has been scorned by liberal Democrats and the judicial activism of the judges they have appointed" (Republican Party 1996). The 2000 Republican platform complained that "scores of judges with activist backgrounds in the hard-left now have lifetime tenure" (Republican Party 2000). It suggested remedies that included an end to lifetime appointment and impeachment of justices. The 2004 Republican platform continued the assault, complaining that a "handful of activist judges threaten to overturn common sense and tradition" and were threatening "America's dearest institutions and our very way of life" (Republican Party 2004). Although the federal courts of the era were dominated by Republican appointees, there were enough decisions, such as the Ninth Circuit's holding in *Newdow v. U.S. Congress*[24] that the Pledge of Allegiance violated the First Amendment, or the Supreme Court's gay rights ruling in *Lawrence v. Texas*,[25] to give continued impetus to the conservative critique of "liberal judicial activism."

In contrast, Democratic platforms of the period did not contain similar objections to judicial activism. Most did not mention the judiciary, although the 2000 platform contained a limited defense of the judiciary and opposition to any legislation that would strip the federal courts of jurisdiction over particular disputes. Yet on the brink of leaving office, President Clinton

---

24. 328 F.3d 466 (9th Cir. 2002), *rev'd,by Elk Grove Unified School Dist. v. Newdow*, 542 U.S. 1(2004).

25. 539 U.S. 558 (2003).

warned of "a new form of ultra-conservative judicial activism that rejects the Government's rights or authority to protect the rights of our citizens and the interests of our citizens"(Clinton 2000). The 2004 Democratic platform contained no direct attack on judicial activism, but the political tables on the issue were turning. The platform expressed concern over the direction that the Court could take under the Bush presidency.

Even outside the confirmation context, members of Congress have displayed similar concerns about judicial activism. One study examined references to "legislating from the bench" in Congress from 1990 to 2006 (Peabody 2007, 196). The author found 127 such references, with over 75% of the references made by Republicans. In Congress, judicial activism is typically viewed as a liberal tool to remake society. In a debate over a federal "marriage protection act" in 2004, for example, Texas Representative Lamar Smith declared that judicial activism had "reached a crisis," as judges "routinely overrule the will of the people, invent so-called rights and ignore traditional values" (U.S. House 2004, 7825). Debating the same bill, Representative Steve Buyer of Indiana declared that "judicial activism has continued to attack the traditions that have defined this Nation—our pledge of allegiance declared unconstitutional—and now it seems that marriage is its next target" (U.S. House 2004a, 6580). Similarly, Senator Hatch stated during a hearing:

> I have for some time now been speaking out against what I have seen as a rising tide of judicial activism because, in my view, the problem of judicial activism is not just an abstract question for legal theorists, but in fact is one of the most important policy issues of the day.
>
> The reason is simple: When unelected, life-tenured judges decide cases based on their own policy preferences, instead of what the law requires, they remove entire spheres of policymaking [*sic*] from the democratic political process. This strikes at the heart of constitutionalism and ultimately undermines our very system of democratic government (quoted in George 2000, 508).

To examine the degree of congressional interest in judicial activism over time, we counted mentions of the phrase in the *Congressional Record*. As with the press counts, we did not distinguish between types of references to judicial activism but simply calculated the number of times the phrase was found per year. The results are shown in Figure 2.

The dramatic spike of mentions in 1997 is not associated with any particular event but reflects some Republican resistance to Clinton nominees to

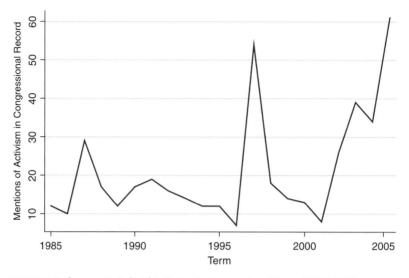

FIGURE 2 References to Judicial Activism in Congressional Record 1985–2005

the federal courts, and is due in part to a congressional hearing of that year on judicial activism (U.S. Senate 1997). At this hearing, Senator Ashcroft argued that "judicial activism strikes at the heart of our system of separation of powers and it represents a real and, I believe, a tangible threat to the people's freedom to govern themselves"(U.S. Senate 1997, 1). Senator Mark Pryor likewise decried judicial activism as a "threat to constitutional democracy" (U.S. Senate 1997, 70).

In more recent years, liberals in Congress have begun to express concern for judicial activism. Senator Joe Biden complained that the pattern of "conservative judicial activism" in striking federal statutes was "more than six times the rate over the history of our Republic" (U.S. Senate 2006, 334). Senator Hillary Clinton objected that Justice Alito had adopted "an unnecessarily narrow view of the Constitution or of our laws to reach a desired outcome" (U.S. Senate 2006a, 3507). The "reinvigoration of Federalism" was described as the "hallmark agenda of the judicial activism of the Rehnquist Court" (U.S. Senate 2005, 10395-06). Senator Carl Levin declared that "the most serious danger lies in the rise of conservative judicial activism, by which the interpretation of the Constitution by some Federal judges has come to overlap with the ideology of right wing politicians"(U.S. Senate 2005a, 10481). Nevertheless, conservative complaints about judicial activism remain predominant, and the gay rights decisions and the prospect of gay marriage gave rise to another hearing on judicial activism before the Senate Judiciary Committee in 2004 (U.S. Senate 2004).

4. The Academic Debate

The discussion of judicial activism in the public domain has a parallel in the academic community, where the arguments for and against activism have an extensive history. The origins of the debate are often linked most prominently with James Bradley Thayer, who, writing in the late nineteenth century, cautioned against the Court's exercise of the power of judicial review to strike federal statutes (Thayer 1893). Thayer argued that the language of the Constitution was inevitably indeterminate and subject to differing interpretations. In light of this uncertainty, he believed that the Court should defer to the legislature's interpretation, so long as it was a reasonable one.[26]

Thayer and subsequent scholars have presented a variety of justifications for this position, but a primary argument centers on the "counter-majoritarian difficulty," reflecting the conundrum posed for democracy when unelected judges encroach on the powers and prerogatives of popularly elected and accountable officials via the exercise of judicial review. According to Thayer and his devotees, when the words of the Constitution are ambiguous, an unelected judiciary should not override the preferences of an elected legislature. Not only was Thayer concerned about the theoretical implications raised by counter-majoritarian decisions, he was also concerned that the elected institutions would become preoccupied with whether the judiciary would approve their policies rather than rely on their own evaluations of the legislation's wisdom and constitutionality. For Thayer, this indirect effect had significant practical implications for democratic action. He also worried that judicialization would lead the legislature to ignore constitutional constraints in deference to judicial review. Even when the Court is correct, the net effect is a negative one, as it causes the democratic branches to shirk their responsibilities to the Constitution. According to Thayer, judicial protection of constitutional principles "may actually contribute to their downfall" (Wolfe 1997, 109).

The counter-majoritarian difficulty highlighted by Thayer has come to preoccupy legal academics. As Suzanna Sherry has written, the counter-majoritarian difficulty is the "central theme in constitutional scholarship," such that "reconciling judicial review and democratic institutions is the goal of almost every major constitutional scholar writing today" (Sherry 2001, 921).

---

26. It is claimed that from the nation's beginning, "it was widely understood that to the extent the federal courts had authority to declare void acts of Congress, they could properly do so only when the constitutional violation was quite clear" (Caminker 2003).

In a series of influential articles, Barry Friedman has documented the history of this debate, concluding that the "academic obsession" with judicial review is, in fact, nothing more than a debate between scholars with differing preferences over certain case outcomes (*e.g.*, Friedman 2002).

Modern scholarship addressing the counter-majoritarian nature of judicial review can be traced to work by Alexander Bickel, perhaps the best-known advocate of judicial restraint. Writing at the time the Warren Court was handing down its dramatic rulings, Bickel observed:

> The root difficulty is that judicial review is a countermajoritarian [*sic*] force in our system . . . . [W]hen the Supreme Court declares unconstitutional a legislative act or the action of an elected executive, it thwarts the will of representatives of the actual people of the here and now; it exercises control, not on behalf of the prevailing majority, but against it (Bickel 1962, 16–17).

Like Thayer, Alexander Bickel contended that the core problem associated with judicial review was that it was a counter-majoritarian governmental force and hence a deviant institution in our democratic system of government. Yet this result was not purely negative for Bickel, who saw value in a politically insulated judiciary that could "appeal to men's better natures, to call forth their aspirations, which may have been forgotten in the moment's hue and cry" (Bickel 1986, 27). Nevertheless, he called for a cautious judiciary that exercised judicial restraint and invalidated statutes only when clearly required by neutral legal principles.

Bickel's call for restraint against the backdrop of the Warren Court's rulings posed a challenge to liberal thinkers who favored those decisions but who were also dedicated to democratic decision making. Laura Kalman has written extensively on how the counter-majoritarian issue confounded liberals (Kalman 1996). As she points out, liberal legal scholars vigorously embraced the Warren Court's rulings on numerous issues but also remembered the long history of conservative rulings from the Supreme Court. Pleased with outcomes produced by the Warren Court, they were nevertheless concerned about their counter-majoritarian character.

More recently, however, the growth of a conservative influence in the judiciary has caused liberals to embrace arguments against a counter-majoritarian judiciary. Prominent examples include Cass Sunstein's call for a minimalist approach to decision making (Sunstein 1999) and Mark Tushnet's suggestion that responsibility for constitutional enforcement be taken from the courts and committed to the elected branches of government (Tushnet 1999). Justice Breyer has similarly suggested that judicial "modesty" should be employed in assessing the constitutionality of legislative enactments (Breyer 2005, 37).

The claims of a counter-majoritarian difficulty are not universally accepted. One response to the counter-majoritarian difficulty is that the elected branches are not truly so majoritarian after all (Choper 1983; Friedman 1993). Certainly, the Senate does not correspond to national majorities, with each state represented equally regardless of its population. The presidential veto authority means that bills passed by a majority of Congress may never become law because they cannot obtain the two-thirds supermajority required for override. Features of the legislative process, such as committee authority, may also prevent a majority-favored bill from being adopted.

These objections to the failure of majoritarianism in the legislature may not reach to the heart of the criticism of judicial activism, however. The U.S. governmental system was created to temper the influence of immediate national majorities, thus preventing majoritarian tyranny. Arguably, objectionable counter-majoritarianism is better viewed as counter-constitutionalism, in which the judiciary assumes legislative authority in violation of constitutional mandates. It is thus more a matter of constitutional separation of powers than of simple majoritarianism. In support of this notion, Judge J. Clifford Wallace has argued that by recognizing the equality of the other branches and stabilizing interbranch relationships, judicial restraint is "consistent with and complementary to the balance of power among the three independent branches" (Wallace 1997, 169).

At the same time, as Thayer was aware, an overactive judiciary may limit the legislature's own attention to constitutional rights. Mark Tushnet has argued that the presence of judicial review creates a "judicial overhang" that distorts legislative protection of the Constitution (Tushnet 1999, 57). Tushnet claims that the backstop of judicial review promotes legislative irresponsibility in promulgating unconstitutional legislation and that it distorts legislators' own constitutional analyses. Legislators themselves appear to recognize this potential for distortion; at least one representative has noted that members of Congress may "take the attitude that we will pass this and let the courts worry about its constitutionality" (U.S. Senate 1997, 142). Indeed, some maintain that the legislature may be superior to the courts in enforcing the U.S. Constitution as it is not only majoritarian but unbound by the limits of litigation and the facts of individual cases (Cross 2000). Thus some have suggested that constitutional federalism concerns are better resolved through democratic "political safeguards" than by judicial intervention that polices the boundaries of state and federal governments (Wechsler 1954).

5. Defending Judicial Activism

While judicial activism surely has its critics, others affirmatively defend the practice. Typically, the defenders challenge claims of judicial activism, arguing that activist decisions are truly consistent with and required by the Constitution. Originalists may go further and contend that the "general theory of constitutional government [as promoted in *The Federalist Papers*] favors judicial activism" (Barber 1988, 836). Oftentimes, defenders stress judicial independence, arguing that the attack on judicial activism is in practice just an assault on the independence of the judiciary.

Although many have supported an active role for the Supreme Court on particular issues, the most explicit embrace of "judicial activism" has been advanced by Arthur Selwyn Miller (A. S. Miller 1984, 167). Miller boldly defends the Court as an oligarchic institution, so long as it makes "sociologically wise decisions" and insofar as "its personnel have the competence to do so" (A. S. Miller 1984, 172). With similar audacity, he argues that all judges are "result-oriented," as are "all commentators upon the work of the judiciary" (A. S. Miller 1984, 173). This, he argues, is good because of the limits of the conventional electoral process. Insulated from this process, the judiciary could be a force for "decency" that would proclaim "affirmative principles of morality" (A. S. Miller 1984, 180). While Miller also emphasizes the limits of judicial authority, he nevertheless clearly views the Court as comprised of wise men (and now women) who should use that authority to generate positive social change.[27] Such an extreme position, however, lacks resonance even within the judiciary itself. As Justice Holmes famously declared, "If my country wants to go to hell, I am here to help it." Likewise, Justice Felix Frankfurter urged that it was not his role to give effect to his theory of what was "wise."[28]

Terri Jennings Peretti has more recently, and more modestly, proclaimed a similar positive role for the judiciary (Peretti 1999). She argues both that the

---

27. Rebecca Brown has similarly suggested that judicial activism offers "a way for a Court to live up to its obligation to serve as a citadel of public justice" (Brown 2002, 1273).

28. *Trop v. Dulles*, 356 U.S. 86, 120 (1958).

Court is ideologically result-oriented in its decisions and that this is good and democratic. The justices are nominated based in significant part on their ideological beliefs and hence are themselves a representative body. Moreover, the Court has seen sufficient turnover that "it can be concluded that the values of the justices mirror and certainly lie within the range of those values currently or recently receiving official representation in other branches of government" (Peretti 1999, 100). She also notes the limitations to majoritarianism in the other branches and suggests that an activist judiciary may itself serve democratic values.

A more recent defense of some level of judicial activism has been propounded by Kermit Roosevelt (Roosevelt 2006), who analyzed historic Supreme Court cases commonly regarded as activist. Many of these cases, he stresses, have become widely accepted as correct. These range from equal protection decisions in *Brown* and *Loving v. Virginia*[29] (invalidating anti-miscegenation statutes), to criminal procedure decisions such as *Miranda v. Arizona*[30] (the recitation of certain rights to those in police custody). Roosevelt recognizes that other activist decisions are less clearly accepted, including those arising from abortion, gay rights, and Establishment Clause cases, among others. Nevertheless, he argues that they were rightly decided and warns that if "the Court adopts a deferential doctrinal test, it will uphold laws that in fact violate the Constitution" (Roosevelt 2006, 174). Ultimately, he suggests that activism is a simplistic term that obscures the crucial question, which is whether the decision is constitutionally correct.

Not all defenses of judicial activism come from liberal quarters. Clint Bolick, writing for the Cato Institute, has called for judicial activism in defense of individual liberties, including property rights (Bolick 2007). Bolick warns that an overly passive judiciary that fails to fulfill its institutional obligation to protect constitutional rights threatens liberty in equal measure to an activist judiciary improperly motivated by its own policy preferences. According to Bolick, deference itself may constitute activism to the extent that it leaves in place legislation that unduly restricts those individual rights. Randy Barnett also defends a conservative judicial activism that would require laws to be carefully scrutinized by judges "and stricken if they violate individual rights—for example, by taking property for public use without paying just compensation" (Barnett 1987, 13).

---

29. 388 U.S. 1 (1967).

30. 384 U.S. 436 (1966).

These defenses of judicial activism focus on the normative justification for the practice and the quality of the decisions it produces in terms of their ability to promote democratic principles. In a sophisticated theoretical treatment of the subject based on a formal model, James Rogers and Georg Vanberg provide a defense of even unprincipled (i.e., politically motivated) judicial activism (Rogers and Vanberg 2007). They explain how such activism can promote better decisions from the legislature whose statutes are reviewed. These authors begin with the premise that the legislature is often less motivated by the best overall policy than by the desire to respond to the desires of the majority's "faction" (ideological or otherwise). The presence of a judicial veto forces the legislature to adopt a broader policy that reflects the interests of other political factions represented on the Court. This "passive" influence of judicial review promotes less factious and more efficient policy making.

Indeed, placing the judiciary in the context of a system of separated powers is important to evaluating judicial activism. One seldom hears complaints of "legislative activism" or "executive activism," but those branches have expanded enormously over our nation's history. The net increase in government activity since the nation's founding is surely greater in the other branches. While the Supreme Court occasionally issues an opinion considered to be activist, the other branches are engaging every day in governmental responsibilities far beyond those contemplated at the founding. Activism might thus be seen simply as the courts' efforts to "retain a proportionate influence over the growing responsibilities of legislative and administrative institutions" and to preserve the tripartite separation of government powers created by the Constitution (Powers and Rothman 2002, 8). The more powerful the other branches, the more risk that they will transcend constitutional or other legal limitations.

6. Is the Court Counter-Majoritarian?

As Barry Friedman cogently points out, where the rubber meets the road with respect to the counter-majoritarian difficulty is whether the Court actually does act to counter the majority will. This question can only be answered via analyses of the justices' actual behavior in exercising the power of judicial review. In his seminal paper examining the Court's decisions to invalidate federal enactments, Robert Dahl concluded that, at least until the 1950s, the justices generally voted to strike only those statutes that had been enacted by previous national majorities no longer in power (Dahl 1957). In contrast, they generally voted to uphold statutes that were preferred by the dominant democratic majorities at the time of the Court's decisions. Later research questioned this conclusion in connection with Warren Court rulings, but even then, the Court acted mainly to invalidate state or local legislation that may not have been popular at the national level (Casper 1976).

Indeed, the Supreme Court is not truly an unaccountable elite institution that imposes its will on the public. Lacking both the power of the purse and of the sword, the Court is dependent on the other branches and on public support for the effectuation of its rulings. As Justice O'Connor pointed out in her opinion in *Planned Parenthood v. Casey*, which was joined by Justices Kennedy and Souter, the Court must render "principled decisions under circumstances in which their principled character is sufficiently plausible to be accepted by the nation."[31] The Court is thus at least somewhat constrained by majoritarian preferences. A prominent critic of judicial activism, Steve Calabresi, has concluded that the Court's power is permitted to persist "because Congress, following popular opinion, actually likes or is at least ambivalent about the policy results being arrived at" (Calabresi 2004, 577).

Surveys of public attitudes toward the judiciary support the notion that the public has a high degree of confidence in the Supreme Court, which is commonly viewed more favorably than Congress or the Presidency (*see* J. M. Jones 2008). Moreover, rigorous research suggests that the courts have been attentive to the views of the public. An analysis of Supreme Court opinions issued between 1956 and 1989 found that the Court was "highly responsive to majority opinion" (Mishler and Sheehan 1993). Moreover, evidence suggests that, throughout its history, the Court's opinions have been influenced by public opinion (Wilson 1993). A study of post-New Deal decisions overturning legislation and protecting minority rights found that these results were consistent with national public opinion and that the Court refused to act when that was not the case (Barnum 1985). One comparative analysis found that the "modern Court appears neither markedly more nor less consistent with the polls than are other policy makers" (T. R. Marshall 1989, 80). This conclusion applies to decisions considered activist, as the research found that relatively unpopular precedents were more likely to be overturned than were more popular ones (T. R. Marshall 1989, 167–185).

---

31. 505 U.S. 833, 866 (1992).

These findings create something of a paradox. While the purportedly "activist" opinions commonly agree with public preferences, the public generally dislikes judicial activism. This is evident both from polling data and from the political use of the concept. Judicial activism would not be wielded as a political epithet if it did not have political value. To some degree, this may reflect a process value—our government is not only "for" the people, it is to be "of" and "by" the people, and the latter attributes favor decision making by the more accountable branches of government. Few complain of sincere judicial enforcement of the commands of the Constitution. The objection is when the justices place their personal policy preferences over those of the legislature without regard to constitutional or other legal demands. What "distinguishes the most activist Courts and justices is the use of some philosophical system that, they say, directs the course of law and judicial action" (Schick 1984, 48). Thus it was a devotion to laissez-faire capitalism that directed the rulings of the pre-New Deal Court and a social libertarianism that produced many of the Warren Court rulings called activist.

⁂ E. Conclusion

Judicial activism has maintained a prominent position in our political and academic lexicon since the 1950s. Fueled by concerns over counter-majoritarian decisions, politicians and academics have focused their attention on the Court's decisions that supplant the will of the electorate as expressed through their representatives. At the same time, activism has been used often as an epithet to criticize the substantive outcome of decisions with which observers disagree. The problem then lies in finding a rigorous definition of the term. To that end, we turn in the next chapter to a more careful theoretical discussion of the concept, with the aim of identifying dimensions to activism that may be evaluated empirically.

TWO

Identifying Judicial Activism

CHAPTER 1 ILLUSTRATES THE SIGNIFICANCE of claims of judicial activism in political discourse. Unfortunately, the debates over judicial activism have "become increasingly acrimonious and destructive," but have failed to shed much light on the true meaning of the concept (Young 2002, 1140). Thus,

> [a]ctivism is one of those "-isms" hurled in anger, in frustration, in condemnation. Like any other slur it is intended to sting, to discredit. In truth, however, it has more of the ring of 'your mother wears combat boots' than of a genuine critique (Brown 2002, 1257).

Yet claims of judicial activism need not be meaningless. One can clearly imagine relatively more or less activist judiciaries that play a greater or lesser role in national governance. At some level, then, evaluating judicial activism requires some means of identifying its presence that is amenable to measurement and evaluation. This chapter sets forth a theoretical and empirical approach to identifying judicial activism in the U.S. Supreme Court.

※ A. Does the Term "Judicial Activism" Have Meaning?

While criticisms of judicial activism have been rampant over the years, the concept has been ill-specified. The absence of clear guidelines for identifying activism has been attributed to the fact that "[t]he critical elements of judicial activism either are subjective or defy clear and concrete definition" (O'Scannlain 2004). Others have concluded that activism defies precise definition because it means different things to different people, having been "defined in a number of disparate, even contradictory ways" (Kmiec 2004, 1443). Furthermore, writers "persist in speaking about the concept without defining it" (Kmiec 2004, 1443), perhaps because critics commonly cry activism whenever they personally disagree with a judicial decision. Erwin Chemerinsky has the "sense that judicial activism is simply the label used for decisions one does not like" (Chemerinsky 2002, 2019). It frequently serves as a "judicial put-down, a polemical, if unenlightening, way of expressing strong opposition to a judicial decision" (S.F. Smith 2002, 1077).[32]

This indeterminacy is reflected in judicial assessments of the term as well. Justice Robert Jackson observed that "[e]very justice has been accused of legislating and every one has joined in that accusation of others" (R.H. Jackson 1955, 80). Judge Frank Easterbrook has argued that the term is an "empty" one (Easterbrook 2002, 1401), while Justice Scalia has decried criticisms of judicial activism as "nothing but fluff" (Scalia 2002, A13). At her confirmation hearings, Justice Ginsburg suggested that judicial activism was a "label too often pressed into service by critics of court results rather than the legitimacy of court decisions" (quoted in Zeigler 1996, 1367–1368).

Nevertheless, the simple fact that a term is misused or only used vaguely does not mean that it lacks intrinsic meaning or value. "Judicial activism" captures an important aspect of modern governance. In this sense, judicial activism is like judicial independence: a concept that is difficult to define and measure but one that is nevertheless a worthy subject of academic attention and evaluation. With respect to the concept of judicial independence, its importance to the rule of law and democratic governance cannot be gainsaid. And we know that an independent judiciary must be "impartial," "politically insulated," and "institutionally legitimate" (Larkins 1996, 611). But what do those terms mean exactly, in practice? Measuring independence can be difficult because of the distinction between *de facto* independence and *de jure* independence: formal independence protections in constitutions and statutes may have little effect when other environmental and behavioral factors conspire to reduce courts' neutrality, insularity, and legitimacy (Hayo and Voigt 2007). Moreover, where does one draw the line between sufficient independence for effective governance and too much independence? In his insightful study of judicial institutions in Latin America, for example, William Prillaman identified instances in which excessive institutional independence led judiciaries toward an arrogant disregard for the rule of

---

32. As Rebecca Brown has noted, currently, the "charge of activism actually distorts constitutional debate and harms important efforts such as the selection of good judges, the development of good theory, and the writing of good opinions," as well as impeding "the public assessment of a court's work by riveting attention on characteristics that are not germane to thoughtful analysis" (Brown 2002, 1259).

law (Prillaman 2000). A report on judicial independence for the Asian Development Bank explains the problem of defining judicial independence this way: "Judicial independence . . . is not something a judicial system 'has' or 'does not have.' Rather, a judicial system may have 'more of it' or 'less of it'" (Asia Foundation 2003). Yet the difficulties associated with (a) defining judicial independence and (b) identifying its optimal levels do not undermine the importance of the enterprise.

Similarly, one might argue that, like independence, judges may display "more" or "less" activism at different times and in different places (Rosenberg 1992).[33] Comparative studies of courts have widely noted the "judicialization" of politics across developed and developing nations alike (Tate and Vallinder 1997; Hirshl 2007; Shapiro and Stone Sweet 2002). These studies often demonstrate how national courts—especially those tasked with either abstract or concrete powers of judicial review[34]—become increasingly involved in policy making, and that members of the legislative branch often enforce the judicialization of politics within individual countries (Langfred 1994). Across nations and across time, therefore, the extent of judicial independence and the scope of judicial policy making has varied. Similarly the activism of the U.S. Supreme Court has waxed and waned over its history (Schick 1984). Thus activism is best conceptualized in terms of a continuum between activism and restraint, with justices or courts compared in terms of gradations along that contiuum.

We make no claims about whether a position between the two poles of activism and restraint is normatively appropriate. Some may believe that the activist or restraintist behaviors of certain justices are more or less justified. Rather, we seek to place justices on a continuum between activism and restraint with no assumptions about where an optimal position lies. As Ernest Young has commented, activism and restraint "connote directions on the continuum between judicial passivity and hegemony. Movement in a particular direction carries no normative weight unless we can explain why that movement has gone too far" (Young 2002, 1163). Such a determination often requires subjective jurisprudential judgments about the interpretation

---

33. Rosenberg highlights the important relationship between judicial activism and independence: independence is a positive attribute for those who favor an activist judiciary, a negative one for those who favor a more restrained one (Rosenberg 1992, 370).

34. The abstract power of judicial review enables a judiciary to review the constitutionality of legislation prior to its implementation; concrete judicial review allows the judiciary to consider legislation's constitutionality only after it has been applied in particular cases.

of legal texts or about the proper role of the judiciary in governance; and those judgments, in turn, often depend on one's unique policy perspectives.

We also begin with the assumption that activism is a multifaceted concept. Because commentators often disagree over whether one or another particular decision is truly activist based on their perspectives on the appropriate interpretation of the Constitution or the impact of a particular decision, we prefer instead to evaluate the justices' activism *across multiple cases* and *using multiple dimensions*. In the chapters that follow, we focus our attention on this systematic data over the course of the justices' careers on the Supreme Court from the 1953 to the 2004 terms.

※ B. Dimensions of Activism

Several scholars have sought to identify specific dimensions associated with judicial activism. Although these dimensional analyses all differ in identifying the relevant dimensions, their elements may be grouped into four general categories: (1) majoritarianism and deference to elected branches; (2) precedential stability and legal fidelity; (3) institutional aggrandizement; and (4) result-oriented judging or policy making. These categories, and the corresponding dimensions identified in the four studies on which we primarily rely (Canon 1983; Marshall 2002; Young 2002; and Cohn and Kremnitzer 2005),[35] are set forth in Table 1.

1. Majoritarianism and Deference to Other
Governmental Actors

All commentators seem to agree that activism encompasses the situation in which a court chooses not to defer to decisions made by other governmental actors, reflecting as it does the counter-majoritarian difficulty discussed in Chapter 1. Deference to other government agents is "probably the most frequent criterion in assessing Supreme Court activism" (Canon 1983, 240); Judge Richard Posner argues that this definition of activism should be

---

35. Not included in Table 1 are five additional items that Cohn and Kremnitzer add to their list: (1) legislative reaction to the decision; (2) administrative reaction; (3) judicial reaction; (4) public reaction; and (5) intervention in non-human rights value disputes (Cohn and Kremnitzer 2005, 347–348, 352).

TABLE 1 Dimensions of Judicial Activism

Category	Canon (1984)	Young (2002)	W.P. Marshall (2002)	Cohn and Kremnitzer (2005)
Deference to Other Branches/ Governments	Majoritarianism	Second-Guessing Federal or State Governments	Counter-Majoritarianism	Majoritarianism and Autonomy
	Substance-Process Distinction	Exercising Broad Remedial Powers	Remedial Activism	Substance-Process Distinction
	Specificity of Policy	Issuing Broad or "Maximalist" Holdings	Judicial Creativity	Broad Holdings
	Availability of Alternative Policy Maker			
Legal Stability	Interpretative Stability	Departing from Precedent	Departing from Precedent	Precedential Stability
	Interpretative Fidelity	Departing from Text/History	Non-Originalism	Interpretative Fidelity to Text/History
Institutional Aggrandizement			Jurisdictional Expansion	Jurisdictional Expansion
				Threshold Liberalization
				Extralegal Rhetoric/Dicta
Results Orientation/ Policy Making		Deciding According to Judicial Policy Preferences		Absence of Clear Rules
				Multiple Opinions

"canonical" (Posner 1996, 320). Canon recognized a distinction, however, between the nullification of an act of Congress or its emasculation through interpretation (which he considered most activist) and the nullification of state and local laws or administrative regulations (which he considered less activist) (Canon 1984, 405). Certainly, challenging the lawmaking authority of a coequal branch of government is among the most consequential acts the justices can perform and thus must take pride of place in any study of judicial activism. This is true for judicial challenges both to legislative enactments and to executive action via administrative agencies. Less significant, but still important, are the justices' decisions to invalidate the acts of the sovereign state governments. These dimensions of activism are not only canonical; they are relatively straightforward to measure empirically using objective criteria.

All four studies described in Table 1 flesh out the notion of counter-majoritarianism by identifying judicial behaviors that do not involve the outright invalidation of enactments or executive regulations, but that nevertheless represent an encroachment on legislative or executive authority. Using varying terminology, the authors note that certain types of decisions or holdings have the potential to "crowd out" or cramp the lawmaking authority of other governmental actors.[36] One such distinction is drawn between decisions that make substantive policy judgments and those that simply protect access to the political process (Canon 1983, 244–245). This distinction is similar to that drawn in the famous footnote four in *Carolene Products*,[37] which gave rise to the theory that judicial review is most properly employed to protect the rights of minority groups whose access to the political process is compromised by their political isolation (Ely 1980). Cohn and Kremnitzer's substance-process distinction is somewhat different: they distinguish between whether a court's decision rests on narrow procedural or broad substantive grounds (Cohn and Kremnitzer 2005, 341). Although these are perhaps valid observations regarding activism, they pose a challenge for epirical measurement. How does one tell, for example, whether a particular decision opens the political process to minorities pursuant to the *Carolene*

---

36. This is not always a "zero-sum game," as it is not necessarily true that "whatever the courts decide, the legislature cannot decide" (Roach 2001, 103). In the case of the U.S. Supreme Court, members of Congress can respond to judicial decisions so as to mitigate the impact of the Court's rulings through statutory provisions that seek to achieve the legislative objective using other legal means (Ignagi and Meernik 1994).

37. *U.S. v. Carolene Products Co.*, 304 U.S. 144, 152 n.4 (1938).

or executive decisions. Yet again, they are not amenable to objective measurement. Distinguishing between cases as maximalist and minimalist is extremely difficult (Posner 1998, 9). Identifying cases according to these broad substantive/procedural or minimalist/maximalist categories requires significant subjective determinations that are not likely to be replicable from one researcher to the next.

2. Interpretative Stability and Fidelity

All four studies also identify a willingness to destabilize precedent as another important dimension to activist decision making. Stare decisis has value in judicial decision making because it promotes stability and predictability in the rule of law and thus the integrity of the judicial process. "Following precedent tends to show that the court is not following the whims of political winds or the judge's own predilections; that is, she is not, in the fashionable phrase, legislating from the bench" (Sinclair 2007, 370). While the choice to disregard existing precedent is not the same as the choice to invalidate the actions of other governmental institutions, it is similar. Instead of refusing to defer to legislatures or executives, votes to overturn precedent reflect a refusal to defer to decisions rendered by prior courts (Young 2002, 1150–1151). Moreover, in doing so, the judge lays bare the choice to create new law in the face of existing, binding legal rules. Overruling precedent is, in short, a judicial repeal. It comes as no surprise, therefore, that justices on the U.S. Supreme Court explicitly overrule precedent only about twice each term (Brenner and Spaeth 1995). As Canon noted, "the most visible and dramatic instance of interpretive instability" involves the Court's explicit overruling of existing decisions, and "[u]sually, the Court is straightforward about it" (Canon 1983, 241). On the other hand, courts can undermine precedent through the gradual erosion of a decision's application to future cases, either by frequently distinguishing a precedent or by simply ignoring it altogether (Hansford and Spriggs 2006). These situations are much harder to identify, of course, than outright votes to overturn a precedent, and thus pose a more difficult (and sometimes perhaps insurmountable) empirical task.

In addition to fidelity to precedent, the four studies also cite as a hallmark of activism a court's failure to display fidelity to text, original intent, or history. Unlike explicit overrulings of precedent, measuring this dimension is fraught with subjective judgments. One need only consider the conflicting opinions in the Supreme Court's recent decision in *District of Columbia v.*

Products footnote approach? One can find process values in many decisions the Court renders, even when those decisions appear to address substantive rights (Posner 1991).

Moreover, where a court is generating broad substantive holdings that affect the rights and obligations of large groups, it more closely resembles the oft-cited "legislating from the bench" about which so many critics complain. This may also be described as "judicial maximalism," and is exacerbated by the imposition of expansive remedies (Young 2002, 1151–1158), especially when the court's ruling precludes an alternative policy maker from deciding the same issue (Canon 1983, 239).

Yet evaluating whether the imposition of certain remedial measures reflects judicial activism is difficult to assess reliably and objectively. In some cases, for example, the choice of remedial measures is largely based on the activities of the defendant. Thus a court could grant an order directing a school district to eliminate discrimination, but the recalcitrant district might refuse to do so. While an ordinary citizen who refuses to obey a judicial order may be found in contempt and jailed, this option may not be feasible for the school district. Consequently, the court "takes over" the district to ensure that its legal ruling is fairly implemented. While this may still be deemed activist, the existence of the broad remedial ruling is as much a function of the litigant's choices and other case circumstances as it is a function of the choices of the judges.

Similarly, all four commentators in Table 1 suggest that activism may lie in broad or "maximalist" holdings or judicial creativity that expands the scope of the court's opinion beyond what is narrowly required to resolve the particular dispute. Indeed, language in judicial opinions may be relatively modest or more ambitious. Activist opinions may be "preachy, with the justices insisting on the full correctness of their position" by giving little quarter to "opposite viewpoints or to the possibility that the justices . . . may be making the wrong choices" (Schick 1984, 49). Cass Sunstein has created a rough taxonomy of this phenomenon. He describes some justices as "minimalists"; minimalist judges are those whose goal is to decide cases but not great philosophical legal questions and who are more respectful of precedent and chary of making large changes in the existing state of the law (Sunstein 1999). According to Sunstein, however, other justices are fundamentalists devoted to the one true original understanding of the Constitution, or they are perfectionists who believe that the Constitution provides only general principles that courts must further (Sunstein 2005, 31–40).

These considerations involving broad versus minimalist holdings move beyond the simple enumeration of votes to invalidate legislative enactments

Heller,[38] involving whether the Second Amendment protects an individual right to bear arms, to appreciate that reasonable people can disagree over original intent or the text of the Constitution. It is noteworthy that the *Dred Scott* decision, today considered classically activist by both liberals and conservatives, was centrally grounded in an originalist interpretation of the Constitution. Chief Justice Taney wrote that the Constitution "speaks not only in the same words, but with the same meaning and intent with which it spoke when it came from the hands of its framers, and was voted on and adopted by the people of the United States."[39] Yet this is the decision held out by Chief Justice Roberts as the prime case of judicial activism. A similar paean to originalism can be found in decisions of the pre-New Deal Court striking federal statutes,[40] decisions now widely held to be inappropriately activist. Reliance on an interpretive theory such as originalism as a cue for judicial activism is thus impossible to replicate with any reasonable expectation of high inter-coder agreement.

3. Institutional Aggrandizement

Two of the studies summarized in Table 1 note yet another possible dimension of judicial activism that is seldom explored but which is also important: the simple expansion of judicial institutional authority to hear cases and controversies. Although at first blush this may appear less of a counter-majoritarian concern, it nevertheless has the potential to crowd out legislative or executive judgments in particular cases. Consider *Baker v. Carr*.[41] In *Baker*, the Supreme Court overruled *Colgrove v. Green*,[42] and held that state legislative reapportionment constituted a justiciable (i.e., resolvable) issue in the federal courts. Until that point, the Supreme Court had deferred to state legislatures on the matter of redistricting as a "political question" inappropriate for judicial resolution. By expanding the power of federal courts to hear these cases, the Court correspondingly reduced the power of state legislatures to determine the shape of their own legislative districts. *Baker* was

---

38. 554 U.S. __, 128 S.Ct. 645 (2008).

39. 19 Howard 393, 426 (1857).

40. *E.g., United States v. Butler*, 297 U.S. 1, 62–63 (1936).

41. 369 U.S. 186 (1962).

42. 328 U.S. 549 (1946).

decided by a liberal majority during the Warren Court. But it is not only liberal justices who vote to expand plaintiffs' access to the federal courts. In *Shaw v. Reno*,[43] the conservative justices of the Rehnquist Court granted access to white plaintiffs who sought to challenge the racial composition of legislative districts in North Carolina, in effect allowing them to challenge affirmative action in the process of legislative redistricting. Access decisions may therefore turn on which parties are most favored by the individual justices (Marshall 2002, 1237–1238).

Both Marshall (2002) and Cohn and Kremnitzer (2005) recognize jurisdictional expansion and threshold liberalization (the lowering of doctrinal thresholds to allow more cases into court) as components of judicial activism. Justiciability doctrines such as standing, mootness, and ripeness limit access to the courts by limiting the types of disputes they can resolve, usually because the complaining party has failed to demonstrate an injury that may be redressed through a judicially imposed remedy. These limitations—or "passive virtues," as Bickel (1962) labeled them—stem from the constitutional constraints that restrict federal judicial review to actual live "cases" and "controversies," as well as from certain "prudential" doctrines developed by the Court to insulate the federal judiciary from deciding political questions better left for resolution by the elected branches. Like other constitutional restrictions or legal doctrines, however, justiciability doctrines often present rather vague standards. Not surprisingly, justices have differed in their interpretation of these constraints; those taking a more liberalizing approach to the doctrines, and thereby allowing more litigants into court, might be considered more activist.

Activism might also be found in the simple decision to add cases to the Supreme Court's docket. The Supreme Court has almost total discretion over its own docket and can decide which appeals it will take for review through the process known as issuing the writ of certiorari. Over the years, the size of the Court's overall docket has varied considerably (Cross and Lindquist 2006, 1697). By accepting *certiorari* on more cases, the Court intrinsically expands its overall legal authority, which could be considered a form of activism. Over the course of the Warren, Burger, and Rehnquist Courts, the docket initially expanded but more recently has contracted (especially under Chief Justice Rehnquist) to fewer than 100 cases a year decided with written opinion.

---

43. 509 U.S. 630 (1993).

4. Result-Oriented Judging

The criteria set forth above all share one element at their core: a concern that via counter-majoritarian actions, interpretive infidelity, or institutional aggrandizement, the Court will exercise its authority to impose the justices' own vision of good public policy on the nation. The trouble with identifying activism in the sense implied by the phrase "legislating from the bench," however, is that some decisions may be so clearly legally justified that no observer would complain about the Court's action. Virtually all would agree, for example, that if the Congress passed a law legalizing human slavery or expropriating all private property, the Court *should* strike it down as contrary to the Constitution. Such an action might be activist in some sense, but it is not the sense used by critics. In that respect, activism inheres in the structural enterprise of judicial review. The true complaint is about striking down legislation as unconstitutional when it is done to further judges' personal policy preferences.

It is this latter view of judicial activism that has caused the question to degenerate into one of mere political disagreement. Conservatives and liberals have their own views about the meaning of the Constitution and quickly declare activist those judicial decisions that differ from their personal policy preferences. Yet this says much about the speaker who criticizes judicial activism and relatively little about the judicial decision itself. Attacks on judicial activism often turn out "to be little more than a rhetorically charged shorthand for decisions the speaker disagrees with" (Roosevelt 2006, 3). If we are to find a meaningful measure for judicial activism, it must be one that is not contingent on the critic's personal ideology.

Nevertheless, there must be some means to distinguish judicial activism from legitimate enforcement of the Constitution. This need not involve privileging a *particular* legal principle, but it requires that the decisions be based on a legal principle and not a political one. Learned Hand's 1958 lectures complaining of Warren Court activism stated that the Court would employ a "protective veil of adjectives . . . to disguise what they are doing and impute to it a derivation far more impressive than their personal policy preferences, which are all that in fact lie behind the decision" (quoted in Keck 2004, 56–57). Judicial activism is, foremost, a measure of decisions rendered according to judges' personal ideologies rather than neutral dictates of the law.

Black's Law Dictionary thus defines judicial activism as a "philosophy of judicial decision-making whereby judges allow their personal views about public policy, among other factors, to guide their decisions" (Garner 2004).

Judge Stanley Birch has likewise declared that an activist judge is "one who decides the outcome of a controversy before him or her according to personal conviction, even one sincerely held, as opposed to the dictates of the law as constrained by legal precedent and, ultimately, our Constitution."[44] Justice Brennan declared in one decision that the majority's analysis was "completely result oriented and represents a noteworthy exercise in the very judicial activism that the Court so deprecates in other contexts."[45] Similarly, Chief Justice Roberts declared in his confirmation hearings that saying that a judge is "result oriented" is "about the worst thing you can say about a judge" (U.S. Senate 2005b, 267).

Moreover, ideologically motivated or preference-driven judicial decision making implicates separation of powers concerns because it potentially involves the judiciary stepping outside its constitutional role, exercising powers more properly exercised by the elected branches. The obvious instance of such an improper aggrandizement of judicial power would involve striking down a statute approved by a majority of elected representatives of the people simply because the justices disagree with the statutes' policy outcomes on ideological rather than legal grounds.[46] "A judge's view of the law may be esteemed; a judge's view on policy is worth no more than any other" (Wilkinson 2008, 75). This criticism goes beyond the straightforward separation of powers concern, however, as it also applies to the overturning of the Court's own precedents. If the Court overrules one of its prior precedents simply because that decision is less ideologically attractive to the current Court majority, such an action is likewise result-oriented.[47] Thus an activist decision is one where "the judge has an ulterior motive for making the ruling" (Kmiec 2004, 1476).

The argument that the Court engages in such result-oriented decision making is amply supported by empirical evidence. Numerous studies of the

---

44. *Schiavo ex rel. Schindler v. Schiavo*, 404 F.3d 1270, 1271 (11th Cir. 2005) (Birch, J., concurring in denial of rehearing en banc).

45. *Engle v. Isaac*, 456 U.S. 107 (1982) (Brennan, J., dissenting).

46. We do not mean to imply by this discussion that we believe that legal judgments can ever be strictly separated from policy judgments. But where the justices' voting behavior corresponds systematically to a particular policy preference, it suggests that the justices' overriding motivations stem from their ideologies on the substantive outcome of certain cases, rather than on a more neutral assessment of the legal issues raised.

47. This pattern has been clearly demonstrated in previous research, particularly in work by Brenner and Spaeth (1995) and Hansford and Spriggs (2006).

justices' voting patterns have demonstrated the influence of ideology on the justices' votes. Advanced most prominently by Segal and Spaeth (1993, 2002), this "attitudinal model" of the justices' behavior has enabled researchers to predict about three-quarters of the justices' votes based on ideology alone. In this regard, Segal and Spaeth argue that judicial restraint is largely a myth. In their study of decisions invalidating legislative enactments, for example, they found that votes to strike legislation largely corresponded with the justices' preferences regarding the substantive policy advanced by the statute under review. With the possible exception of Rehnquist, they concluded that "all of the justices clearly appear to use restraint—along with judicial activism—as a means to rationalize, support, and justify their substantive policy concerns" (Segal and Spaeth 1993, 326). Considerable additional research has confirmed these findings. (Much of this research and its implications are summarized in Cross (1997).)

This ideological effect is made plain from research on the decisions of Justice Frankfurter, often considered an apostle of judicial restraint but whose apparent dedication to a neutral principle is not supported by the data. In his decisions involving review of state action regulating business and labor, Frankfurter did not demonstrate an across-the-board commitment to defer to legislative judgments. Rather, Frankfurter's post-New Deal voting demonstrated a clear ideological bias for conservative outcomes (Spaeth 1964). While he consistently affirmed anti-union regulations, for example, he often voted to strike down government restraints on business. According to Spaeth (1964), therefore, his actual voting practices were more ideological than restraintist.

On the other hand, while Segal and Spaeth present persuasive evidence of ideological judging on the Supreme Court, they fall far short of explaining all the justices' votes. Numerous opinions are unanimous, even though the justices vary considerably in their ideological preferences. Conservatives reach liberal results and liberals, conservative ones, and "vote patterns simply cannot be explained by the justices' policy preferences alone" (Keck 2004, 271). A study of statutory invalidations found a distinct ideological effect but conceded that it "left significant variance unexplained" (Howard and Segal 2004, 142). One other study documents the substantial minority of cases in which the justices' voting patterns display "disordered" voting, i.e. when the justices deviate from their typical liberal-conservative alignment (Edelman, Klein and Lindquist 2008). Perhaps there is an inevitable temptation to affirm political decisions that one favors ideologically, but justices may resist this temptation to a greater or lesser degree. Those who show less resistance may be considered more result-oriented.

The idea of result-oriented judging is also reflected in at least two of the studies summarized in Table 1. Both Young (2002) and Marshall (2002) discuss "partisan activism," reflecting decisions in which the justices favor particular parties or politicians. This form of result-oriented decision making is far more extreme than the type that simply favors particular policy outcomes, as it favors the specific parties (or presidents) with whom the justices are affiliated. But Cohn and Kremnitzer (2005) also discuss other elements of activist decision making that have a distinct policy dimension. Where the court "expand[s] its opinion beyond the requirements of a particular case" via obiter dicta, for example, it may be a sign that the court is expressing its "self-perceived role as active participant in social, and possibly political, spheres" (Cohn and Kremnitzer 2005, 342). This perspective implicitly incorporates the idea that judges act outside their proper role when they primarily decide cases according to their own personal policy preferences.

Finally, the importance of result-oriented judging to claims of judicial activism has been recently discussed by two conservative judges in connection with the Supreme Court's decision in the gun control case *District of Columbia v. Heller*.[48] In a law review article examined on the front page of the *New York Times,* Judge J. Harvie Wilkinson III notes the importance of the appearance of neutrality in judicial decision making and argues that the justices must set aside their policy preferences or else threaten the law's legitimacy (Wilkinson 2008). He is particularly concerned when the justices vote to strike legislative enactments on the basis of their own policy preferences regarding the underlying substantive policy at issue: "when a court appears to be exercising [its] discretion in a way that arguably accords with the political preferences of the judges in the majority—as was the case in *Heller*—more members of the public lose faith in the idea that justice is blind" (Wilkinson 2008, 16). According to Wilkinson, the outcome in *Heller* in particular, in which the Supreme Court struck down the District of Columbia's gun control law as violative of the Second Amendment, ignored principles of separation of powers and federalism, as well as the legislature's comparative expertise. In his own critique of the *Heller* decision, Judge Richard Posner makes a similar observation about result-oriented judging: "The absence of principles [that might otherwise constrain constitutional interpretation] supports the hypothesis that ideology drives decisions in cases in which liberal and conservative values collide. If loose construction produces

---

48. 554 U.S. __, 128 S.Ct. 645 (2008).

a conservative limitation on government, most conservatives will support it and most liberals will oppose it; and if it produces a liberal limitation on government, most liberals and conservatives will switch sides" (Posner 2008, 35). Both judges recognize that when decisions appear to be based almost exclusively on the justices' own policy preferences, it suggests a more activist orientation on the Supreme Court.

⅍ B. Empirical Measurement

As discussed above, some—but certainly not all—dimensions of judicial activism are amenable to systematic, large-N studies of judicial voting behavior that rely on quantified measurements. We begin our analysis in Chapter 3 with an evaluation of the first canonical dimension of judicial activism: the justices' votes to invalidate legislative enactments in the federal context. After identifying cases in which the Court considered the constitutional validity of congressional statutes, we assess the individual justices' votes to strike or uphold those statutes during the Warren, Burger, and Rehnquist Courts. In doing so, we also assess the extent to which the justices' votes are driven by their policy preferences, thus incorporating the idea of result-oriented judging into the analysis. In Chapter 4, we conduct the same analysis with respect to state legislative enactments, again assessing how those individual votes are shaped by the justices' ideological orientations. In Chapter 5, we consider the justices' votes to invalidate or uphold the actions of the executive branch at both the federal and state levels, adding consideration of whether those votes further the justices' individual policy preferences as well. Thus, in Chapters 3, 4, and 5, we focus our attention on the counter-majoritarian nature of the justices' decision making by evaluating their conduct in cases challenging actions rendered by the elected branches. Our analysis relies on the United States Supreme Court Judicial Database compiled by Harold Spaeth (Spaeth 2005), supplemented by additional data we collected on our own.

As for institutional aggrandizement, in Chapter 6 we consider the votes of the justices to grant access to the federal courts. As noted, these decisions are appropriately included in our study because they have the potential to result in the enlargement of the judiciary's institutional authority. Like the other measures we evaluate, we assess whether the justices are influenced by their ideological predispositions when they vote to grant or deny access to certain litigants.

Finally, in Chapter 7 we evaluate the individual justices' votes to overturn existing precedent. Fortunately, the Justice-Centered Supreme Court Databases, compiled by Harold Spaeth and Sara Benesh (Benesh and Spaeth 2005), provide the data for us to analyze the individual votes of the justices to overrule precedent. To construct the database, each case was examined to determine whether the individual justices, in dissent or in the majority, voted to reverse precedent. We also evaluate the justices' adherence to precedent in relation to their policy preferences. Do the justices vote to overturn precedent primarily because they disagree with the ideological direction of the doctrine embodied in the existing precedent?

Our analyses therefore rely in part on the frequency of each justice's votes that might be considered activist. However, we go further than simply calculating frequencies to evaluate the ideological pattern of those actions as indicia of result-oriented judicial decision making. Thus we can distinguish justices who are activist in pursuit of a particular ideological agenda.

C. Limitations to a Systematic Empirical Approach

"Judicial activism" is commonly employed simply as a partisan epithet, but we have seen that it does have substantive content of its own, and several (but not all) elements of the concept discussed above are amenable to empirical measurement in a systematic study of the justices' voting behavior across multiple cases. While the law is not always easily reducible to a quantitative metric, political scientists have made some progress in designing simplified measures to capture legal concepts. A study of judicial activism can build upon this foundation. Certain of the elements of judicial activism described by the commentators listed in Table 1 and elsewhere, however, are not easily measured. For our purposes, as described below, we focus on those elements of the concepts that are susceptible to empirical measurement.

Although we cannot measure all aspects of judicial decision making associated with the concept of activism, our intention is not to offer the definitive analysis of judicial activism. Rather, we seek to add evidence that informs the debate. Our objective is to advance the discussion by identifying quantitative measures of activism and assessing the individual justices' behaviors against those metrics. Certainly, large-N studies of judicial voting patterns mask the nuances that may be gleaned from the analysis of individual cases and their contexts; some excellent research exists, such as Howard Gillman's study of the *Lochner*-era Court, which situates activism within its historical and philosophical context (Gillman 1993). We applaud the use of such approaches as they often provide a rich understanding of judicial behavior in particular historical situations. But we also think that applying quantitative analysis to study activism can be illuminating in its own way by revealing patterns of voting behavior across multiple cases and multiple dimensions.

We also recognize that even though we have focused exclusively on those measures that are most amenable to valid and replicable measurement, subjective judgments still creep in to any social scientific study. Most vulnerable to this criticism is our reliance on the ideological direction of the justices' votes to identify result-oriented voting behavior on the part of the individual justices. As we explain in the following chapters, we largely rely on Harold Spaeth's U.S. Supreme Court Database, or on the coding rules he has developed, to identify the ideological direction of the justices' votes or to identify the ideological direction of the substantive policy outcomes promoted by legislative enactments or administrative action. These coding rules have been the subject of some criticism in the literature of late (Harvey 2008; Shapiro forthcoming). Yet the Spaeth Database nevertheless provides the most comprehensive publicly available data source, and it has been used in countless studies to advance our knowledge of the Supreme Court. It also has the benefit of allowing replication of existing studies and is thus the best means available to conduct our chosen study. At this point in time, it quite simply represents the most valid, reliable data available for our purposes.

One final drawback to quantitative analysis of votes has an important impact on our study: not all the justices from the Warren Court served long enough under that chief justice to make analysis of their votes feasible. For that reason, in the analytical chapters, we chose to omit the following justices from our analysis: Justices Burton, Minton, Reed, Whittaker, Jackson, Fortas, and Goldberg. None of these justices served sufficiently long periods on the Court after 1953 to make their records broad enough for meaningful analysis. Even without these justices, however, we are able to compare the voting records of Justices Douglas, Thomas, Black, Kennedy, Brennan, Marshall, Scalia, Souter, O'Connor, Ginsburg, Breyer, Warren, Stewart, Stevens, Rehnquist, Blackmun, Powell, Harlan, White, Burger, Clark, and Frankfurter.

✌ D. Conclusion

Judicial activism is a concept of significance in modern discussions of judicial decision making. For that reason, we have endeavored to identify specific dimensions associated with the concept and describe how some of those dimensions might be measured and evaluated. An empirical study such as this one, however, cannot conclusively establish that a particular decision, justice, or even era of the Court was "inappropriately" activist. Instead, we seek to reveal how different justices display more or less activism in different contexts. Activism and restraint constitute a continuum; our efforts aim at placing the justices along that continuum in comparative perspective.

THREE

Judicial Review of Federal Statutes

THIS CHAPTER BEGINS OUR effort to measure judicial activism quantitatively. As noted in Chapter 2, one of the "canonical" measures of judicial activism involves the Court's invalidation (via the exercise of judicial review) of policies duly enacted by the people's representatives. This counter-majoritarian concern is especially acute when the Court acts to invalidate the actions of Congress, a coordinate branch. Hence we consider the frequency with which the justices vote to declare federal statutes unconstitutional on the Warren, Burger, and Rehnquist Courts. Our measure of judicial activism in this context has two dimensions. First, we simply measure how often the justices voted to strike federal statutes on constitutional grounds. Second, we evaluate the degree to which those votes were driven by the justices' ideological preferences. Where justices consistently vote to uphold conservative statutes but strike liberal ones, or vice versa, it suggests that the justices' decision-making process is driven by their own policy preferences rather than some more neutral method of constitutional interpretation. Because both measures present relevant assessments of judicial activism, we evaluate them together to determine the relative degree of activist decision making manifested by the justices sitting on the Supreme Court between 1953 and 2004.

✹ A. The Standard: Declaring Federal Laws Unconstitutional

As noted above, the paradigmatic case of judicial activism involves the Supreme Court's decision to strike down a federal statute as in violation of the Constitution. By voiding an act of the elected branches, the Court arguably places itself in the position of disrupting the constitutional separation of powers by assuming legislative power. Indeed, in doing so, the Court exercises something like a presidential veto, except that, unlike the President's veto, judicial invalidations cannot be overridden with a two-thirds majority vote in Congress. Rather, to be overridden, the Court's rulings invalidating an act of Congress require the elaborate process of constitutional amendment.

The framers of the Constitution considered providing the judiciary with a broad institutional veto power in the process of legislative enactment. In particular, they debated a proposal from James Madison pursuant to which members of the judiciary would sit in a "Council of Revision" with the authority to veto newly enacted legislation. Ultimately, the proposal failed because the delegates believed that it assigned an inappropriate policy-making role to the judiciary (Anderson 2006). The courts' current exercise of the power of judicial review differs from the power it would have wielded under the Council of Revision proposal, since that proposal would have granted judges the authority to invalidate legislative enactments prior to their actual enforcement. Known as "abstract review," this veto authority has been incorporated into several European constitutional systems (Stone Sweet 2000). In contrast, the federal judiciary has the power to invalidate acts of Congress only after an actual case or controversy has arisen regarding application of the statute. Nevertheless, the exercise of judicial review under the existing Constitution provides the Court with impressive institutional authority to inject itself into the policy-making process by striking laws as unconstitutional.

For that reason, a consensus has emerged that the benchmark measure of judicial activism should be the invalidation of federal legislation. For Judge Richard Posner, a condition for any claim of judicial activism is a decision in which a court acts "contrary to the will of the other branches of government," such as invalidating a legislative statute (Posner 1996, 320). Cass Sunstein contends that "it is best to measure judicial activism by seeing how often a court strikes down the actions of other parts of government, especially those of Congress" (Sunstein 2005, 42–43). Charges of judicial activism "are often leveled when a court strikes down a democratically enacted statute" (Peters 1997, 434). Most political scientists have agreed with this assessment, finding that the "most dramatic instances of a lack of judicial restraint—or conversely the manifestation of judicial activism—are decisions to declare acts of Congress . . . unconstitutional" (Segal and Spaeth 2002, 413).

This view accords with the counter-majoritarian critique of an activist judiciary, and the invalidation of federal legislation seems most objectionable since federal laws represent a form of national consensus regarding appropriate policy. State legislation also has a democratic pedigree, but the application of a state law is limited to a portion of the nation only. Indeed, some state laws, such as the Southern requirements of racial segregation, may be contrary to the national popular will. Thus, in contrast to federal legislation, the invalidation of state legislation is not necessarily counter-majoritarian beyond the given state affected by the Court's action.

Moreover, the actual invalidation of federal statutes may reflect only the tip of the iceberg when it comes to the pragmatic effect of judicial review. When adopting legislation, Congress is aware of the prospect of future judicial review and may modify its actions accordingly. As a result, when faced with an activist judiciary, Congress may simply choose not to pass legislation or pass different legislation than if it were faced with a deferential judiciary (Rogers and Vanberg 2007). This chilling effect on legislative action may be among the most significant consequence of judicial activism, but it is difficult to measure directly. Therefore the number of actual statutory invalidations, and the individual justices' votes in those cases, must form the starting point for our empirical analysis of counter-majoritarianism at the Supreme Court.

⁘ B. Invalidations Over Time

We begin our investigation of the justices' responses to constitutional challenges to federal enactments by examining the Court's pattern of activity over time. To compare the Court's willingness to strike down federal laws, we calculated its propensity to do so over several eras, using data provided by the Congressional Research Service. We categorized the Courts of the twentieth century by chief justice, except that the post-"switch in time that saved nine" Court is referred to as the Roosevelt Court (1937 to 1953).[49] For the Courts with long tenure, we separate the Early Warren Court (1954–1962) from the Late Warren Court (1963–1969) and the Early Rehnquist Court (1986–1994) from the Late Rehnquist Court (1995–2004). For each period, we calculated the annual average rate at which the Court struck down federal statutes, as reported in Figure 3.

---

49. The "switch in time that saved nine" is the catchy phrase that is commonly attached to Owen J. Roberts's switch from conservative to liberal voting in support of Roosevelt's New Deal legislation. Since the Court was closely split, this shift in one vote resulted in the legislation being upheld rather than struck down. Scholars are divided over whether the shift was a response to political pressure brought to bear under Roosevelt's court-packing plan (Cushman 1998).

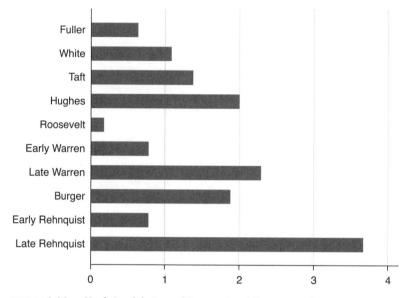

FIGURE 3 Mean Yearly Invalidations of Congressional Enactments, by Court Era

Some obvious patterns emerge. First, later Courts, including the Warren, Burger, and Rehnquist Courts, were generally more activist in striking federal legislation than their predecessors. One exception involves the Hughes Court. Under Chief Justice Hughes (1930–1936), the Court persisted in striking New Deal legislation as in violation of the Due Process Clause. After 1936 and the "switch in time" by Justice Roberts, however, the justices of the "Roosevelt Court" were much more deferential to the Roosevelt Administration's policies. By far the most activist Court by this measure was the Late Rehnquist Court, invalidating almost four acts of Congress per term on average. In comparative terms, the Warren Court does not appear particularly activist, although its later years saw a clear increase in decisions declaring acts of Congress unconstitutional.

Figure 3 presents aggregate data measuring mean invalidations per term. In Figure 4, we present a more nuanced picture of the Court's exercise of judicial review from 1953 to 2004. In particular, we present data on the number of constitutional challenges to federal enactments in each term, and the number of those challenges that were successful (i.e., where the Court struck the statute). This comparison is obviously important: the absolute number of statutory invalidations fails to take into account the number of statutes subject to challenge in any given Court term. Thus, one Court might strike all statutes challenged during a given term on constitutional grounds.

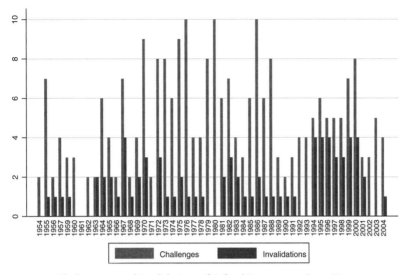

FIGURE 4   Challenges to and Invalidations of Federal Statutes per Court Term

Another court might strike four statutes out of ten challenges, upholding the constitutionality of six federal statutes. Indeed, a court that strikes no statutes in the face of no constitutional challenges is not necessarily restraintist.

This point highlights the importance of the Court's agenda, which depends on decisions made by litigants to bring constitutional challenges in federal court and the Court's willingness to hear them. One potential influence over the Court's docket involved a change in 1988 to the law governing the case selection process. Until that year, the Supreme Court's docket was governed in part by Public Law 86-3 (28 U.S.C. § 1252), which provided for direct appeals to the Supreme Court from decisions invalidating acts of Congress. Public Law 86-3 was repealed in 1988. It is possible that this change influenced the shape of the Court's docket as well as the likelihood that the justices would uphold a challenged enactment (Lindquist and Solberg 2007, 80). Certainly for the period between 1970 and 1988, the Court heard many cases challenging the constitutionality of federal laws, sometimes up to 10 such challenges each year. The mean number of challenges during that period was 6.52, with 21.2% invalidated on average per term. After 1988, the mean number of challenges was 4.70, with an average invalidation rate of 39.6%. Thus, after 1988, the Court heard somewhat fewer challenges to federal statutes but invalidated relatively more statutes.

Even taking this issue into consideration,[50] however, it is clear that since 1953, the Court marched along at a fairly steady pace in terms of federal invalidations until the late Rehnquist Court. The Warren Court heard relatively few challenges and invalidated one or two per term. The Burger Court heard many more challenges, but similarly invalidated about one or two per term. After 1994, however, the Rehnquist Court ramped up the action by invalidating close to four per term. Thus the Rehnquist Court was quite aggressive in its actions toward Congress, especially when one takes into consideration that the Rehnquist Court otherwise substantially limited its docket on certiorari, sometimes taking fewer than 100 cases per year.

Recent research has investigated the dynamics of the Rehnquist Court's invalidation of federal statutes. According to one study, after the 2004 election, in which Republicans took control of Congress, the probability that the Court would strike a liberal federal law rose by 47% (Harvey and Friedman 2006). The authors suggest, therefore, that the Rehnquist Court's willingness to strike congressional enactments may have been empowered or inspired by a conservative mood in the country or a conservative Congress that was unlikely to retaliate against the Court.

𝑀 C. The Voting Behavior of the Individual Justices

Although studying the actions of the Court as a whole provides interesting insights, our purpose is to compare individual justices' voting behavior for

---

50. The impact of the jurisdictional statute should not be overestimated. First, the statute allowed an appeal only in those cases in which the lower court had *invalidated* the congressional enactment. Although a direct appeal from the district court bypasses an appellate bench that might reverse the lower court's invalidation, this fact suggests that these cases might have been granted certiorari in any event, as apparently reasonable minds could differ over the statute's constitutionality. In addition, the mere fact that a case fell under the provisions of the jurisdictional statute did not mean that the Court was required to give the appeal a full hearing. In letters to Congress explaining why the elimination of appeals was appropriate, the justices themselves argued that many appeals were disposed of by using summary procedures as if they were petitions for certiorari. In contrast, the cases in our data were not decided summarily; almost all received oral argument and were decided with opinion. As one recent empirical study has noted, "[T]he 1988 legislative changes thus seem to have had little or no effect on the Court's plenary docket" (Cordray and Cordray 2001). For that reason, while we think this statutory change is worth consideration, it does not undermine the thrust of our analysis. Nevertheless, to address this concern, we consider both the *frequency* of invalidation as well as the *proportion of votes to invalidate* in our analysis.

signs of activism. Justices are regularly confronted with appeals in which the validity of a federal statute is challenged and they must cast votes for or against its constitutionality. Before proceeding with our own analysis, we review the existing research evaluating the justices' behavior in cases challenging the constitutionality of federal laws.

One of the most prominent studies of Supreme Court activism in this context is found in an editorial, rather than in formal research. In 2005, the *New York Times* published an editorial in which Paul Gewirtz and Chad Golder analyzed decisions rendered by the Rehnquist Court invalidating federal laws in the 1994-to-2004 Court terms (Gewirtz and Golder 2005). The researchers found that the most conservative justices were far more likely to vote to strike such laws than were their more liberal colleagues on the bench. On this basis and "at least on this measure," Gewirtz and Golder charged the conservative justices with greater judicial activism (Gewirtz and Golder 2005). In a similar analysis, Lori Ringhand examined the Rehnquist Court during the same period of stable membership. Like Gewirtz and Golder, she found that the conservative justices on the Rehnquist Court were "much more likely than their liberal counterparts to vote to declare federal statutes unconstitutional" (Ringhand 2007, 49). For all the justices, however, she found that votes on the constitutionality of federal statutes were associated with the justices' ideological preferences. Thus Justices Thomas and Scalia were more likely to find a liberal statute unconstitutional, while Justices Stevens and Souter were more likely to find a conservative statute invalid. Segal and Spaeth (2002) made the same general finding, as did Lindquist and Solberg (2006).

We extend these analyses to evaluate the justices' voting behavior over the Warren, Burger, and Rehnquist Courts. Our evaluation focuses on the career scores of the justices sitting on those Courts in terms of their propensity to strike federal statutes. In that regard, our study spans the votes of justices across different "natural courts" (i.e., courts whose membership remains stable) and thus of justices who likely are not hearing the same disputes. Although it may be preferable for some purposes to evaluate decision making only within the time frame of natural courts, this approach also narrows the range of decisions that can be evaluated. This is especially true in the case of challenges to federal statutes, which comprise such a small percentage of the Court's docket. Nevertheless, we remain sensitive to the notion that the Court's agenda changes over time and that, obviously, different statutes were evaluated by different Courts and often by different justices. We return to this point later in this chapter.

1. The Frequency of the Justices' Votes to Strike Federal Statutes

We begin our analysis by considering the frequency with which individual justices voted to overturn a federal statute. These decisions involve a broad range of statutes, as well as unanimous and nonunanimous decisions striking or upholding the statutes at issue. Our data are drawn from the U.S. Supreme Court Judicial Database; however, since that database only identifies cases in which a statute was actually struck, we enhanced the data by identifying cases in which a statute was challenged but ultimately upheld.[51] Thus we are able to incorporate the justices' perspectives in dissent and capture votes in decisions that unanimously upheld the challenged law. The data cover the period between 1953 and 2004.

In Table 2, we present a mean estimate of the frequency with which each justice voted to strike a federal statute for each term that justice served on the Court. This measure does not take into consideration the number of challenges considered by each justice; it simply reflects the number of times he or she voted to strike a federal statute per term. The justices' relative position on this scale is presented in Figure 5.

These data reveal that over the course of his lengthy tenure on the Court, Justice Marshall voted to strike federal statutes most often, averaging more than three such votes per Court term during which he served. Close behind, another liberal justice—William Douglas—voted on average to strike federal statutes almost three times during each term served. Justice Thomas, the conservative justice who replaced Justice Marshall, also demonstrated a propensity to vote to strike federal statutes frequently, doing so on average 2.8 times per term. While Justice Marshall and Justice Thomas obviously did not consider the same cases, they nevertheless voted to invalidate federal legislation at about the same frequency when those challenges were presented. Other conservative justices who voted frequently to invalidate federal legislation were Justices Kennedy and Scalia.

Among the justices least likely to cast a vote to strike federal statutes were Frankfurter, Clark, Burger, and Warren. Frankfurter's average should be

---

51. The "uncon" variable in the Supreme Court Database identifies situations in which a federal, state, or local law was invalidated, but it is coded zero for all other cases. The Justice-Centered Databases identify all votes to declare laws unconstitutional (until 2000 at this time), but otherwise do not identify unanimous decisions in which a statute was challenged and upheld.

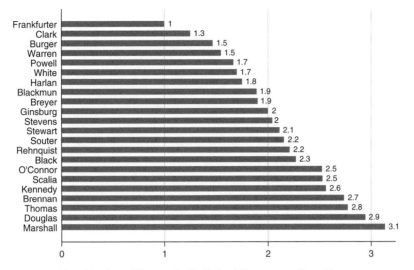

FIGURE 5 Mean Number of Votes to Strike Federal Statutes per Court Term

TABLE 2 Mean Votes to Strike Federal Statutes per Court Term

Justice	Mean Votes to Strike	Number of Votes	Court Terms
Black	2.26	63	1953–1970
Blackmun	1.88	138	1970–1993
Brennan	2.73	166	1956–1989
Breyer	1.90	55	1994–2004
Burger	1.46	108	1969–1985
Clark	1.25	40	1953–1966
Douglas	2.94	84	1953–1975
Frankfurter	1.00	17	1953–1961
Ginsburg	2.00	59	1993–2004
Harlan	1.75	56	1954–1970
Kennedy	2.56	80	1987–2004
Marshall	3.13	135	1967–1990
O'Connor	2.52	121	1981–2004
Powell	1.66	103	1971–1986
Rehnquist	2.20	188	1971–2004
Scalia	2.52	94	1986–2004
Souter	2.15	67	1990–2004
Stevens	2.04	163	1975–2004
Stewart	2.11	114	1958–1980
Thomas	2.76	67	1991–2004
Warren	1.54	49	1953–1968
White	1.70	164	1961–1992

considered with some caution, however, as he served on the Warren Court for only nine terms and considered only 17 challenges to federally enacted legislation during that period. The same might be said of Clark. But Justice Burger's record is far more comprehensive, covering 17 terms and involving 108 challenges to federal statutes. Yet he voted to strike a federal statute only 1.5 times per Court term on average. When it comes to votes to strike federal laws, measured as the average number of votes to strike per term, the record suggests no pattern tracking liberalism with activism. Instead, there are some very liberal justices who are activists, as well as some liberals who demonstrate restraint. The same can be said of the conservative justices on the Court. Activism by this measure reflects a mixed bag ideologically.

To compare the justices further, we also calculated the percentage of votes to strike federal laws based on the number of challenges brought before the Court. This calculation produces a slightly different ranking, as the denominator varies for each justice: some justices considered more challenges than others. The measure thus reflects the justices' willingness to strike *once presented with a challenge*; these values are presented in Figure 6.

According to this standard, Douglas demonstrates the greatest propensity to strike federal laws, as measured by the percentage of votes he cast in cases where the constitutionality of a federal statute was challenged. From the same era on the Warren Court, Justice Black is also more likely than not to strike a federal law challenged before the Court. In later terms, Justices

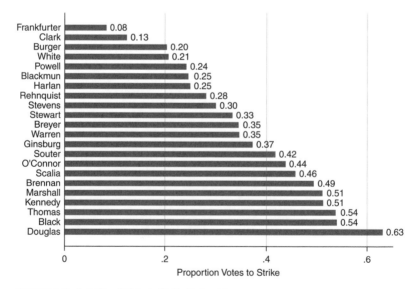

FIGURE 6 Probability of Vote to Strike Federal Law

Kennedy and Thomas also tip the scales in favor of voting to strike federal statutes when those challenges were brought. Far less likely to strike—even when presented with a large number of opportunities to do so—were Justices Burger, White, and Powell. When read in conjunction with the data presented in Table 2 and Figure 5, these initial findings lend credence to charges of judicial activism by both Warren Court liberals and Rehnquist Court conservatives. Of course, these measures present only a partial portrait of the justices' behavior, dependent as they are on the types and number of challenges considered by the justices over the relevant periods. A more telling measure of judicial activism would reflect the extent to which the justices' votes were influenced by their personal policy preferences.

2. The Voting Behavior of the Individual Justices as Influenced by Ideology

Central to our evaluation of activism is the notion of judicial ideology, the source of result-oriented judging. Mere votes to invalidate statutes do not necessarily capture the full measure of judicial activism. Consider a hypothetical justice who is extremely liberal. This justice is by nature also extremely activist, willing to strike conservative legislation aggressively. As it happens, however, the Court chooses to consider or is presented with challenges only to liberal governmental actions. Consequently, our hypothetical justice consistently votes to uphold those actions. Although the justice was by nature highly activist and ideological, his votes make him appear quite deferential. As noted above, this agenda-setting effect may compromise the probative value of vote frequencies or percentages, especially when comparing justices across different time periods. A true measure of activism requires that we isolate the ideological effect.

Beyond simple counting, political scientists have statistically analyzed the tendency of justices to vote to invalidate federal statutes while taking ideology into consideration. Segal and Spaeth evaluated the Rehnquist Court and found that the justices' individual votes to strike federal laws appeared ideologically driven, with liberals voting to strike conservative statutes and conservative justices finding liberal statutes unconstitutional (Segal and Spaeth 2002). Segal and Robert Howard examined cases between 1985 and 1994, in which one of the parties petitioned the Court to invalidate a state or federal law, (Howard and Segal 2004). The authors found that the justices' inclination to strike a statute depended largely on whether a conservative or liberal party urged such an action. Similarly, a study of the Burger and Rehnquist Courts by Lindquist and Solberg found a high level of statistical and substantive correlation between a justice's ideology and his or her decision to strike or uphold a statute (Lindquist and Solberg 2007). This research serves to confirm the claim that Supreme Court decisions and associated activism are often driven by personal policy preference.

To capture this effect, statutory policies must be coded as liberal or conservative. To achieve this, we relied on the U.S. Supreme Court database, which contains coding for the ideological direction of the case's outcome. In general, these codes are intuitive and follow the traditional political interpretation of the issues before the Court. Thus a decision in favor of reproductive rights is coded as liberal, while a decision upholding a statute that restricted such rights would be coded conservative. A decision favoring the constitutional rights of criminal defendants would be deemed liberal, while one favoring the government in a criminal case would be considered conservative. Where a statute was struck and the outcome was coded as liberal, we coded the statute's substantive policy as conservative, and vice versa. Most of the decisions in our data are amenable to such ideological characterization.

As an example, consider the prominent Warren Court decision in *United States v. Robel*,[52] involving a prosecution under the federal Subversive Activities Control Act which made it unlawful for any member of a "Communist-action organization" to be employed at a defense facility, even as a simple machinist. The Court found that the law violated the freedom of association protected by the First Amendment. Four justices joined Chief Justice Warren's majority opinion, and Justice Brennan filed a concurring opinion agreeing with the outcome on somewhat different constitutional grounds (Justice Marshall took no part in the decision). This statute is coded as substantively conservative. Justices White and Harlan dissented from the decision, and thus their votes are coded as votes to uphold a conservative statute.

For a few challenged statutes in our data, however, the Supreme Court database identified no directionality for the case outcome because there was no apparent ideological content to the decision. An example is the line-item veto decision. When Congress enacted a statute allowing the president to nullify certain provisions of appropriations bills, it was challenged as violating constitutional separation of powers principles. In *Clinton v. City of New York*,[53]

---

52. 389 U.S. 258 (1967).

53. 524 U.S. 417 (1998).

the Supreme Court found the law unconstitutional. The ideological import of the law was unclear, however, as its impact would vary depending on the parties controlling Congress and the presidency, respectively. The invalidated statute was pushed by congressional Republicans but supported by President Clinton and numerous Democrats. These few decisions were thus coded as involving statutes with neutral ideological content.

Figure 7 presents a graph reflecting the proportion of the justices' votes to strike liberal and conservative federal enactments. This graph suggests a degree of ideological skewing in the justices' voting patterns. Among the more liberal justices, Douglas demonstrates the greatest difference in his propensity to strike liberal as opposed to conservative statutes. Note that he is more than 80% likely to vote to invalidate a conservative federal law, yet less than 20% likely to do so when a liberal law is challenged. Justices Warren, Black, Brennan, Harlan, and Marshall demonstrate similar tendencies, and to a slightly lesser degree, Justices Ginsburg and Souter. Although they strike more conservative than liberal laws, Justices Breyer, White, Stevens, and Blackmun appear to be more evenhanded in their voting behavior. Among the conservatives, Thomas, Scalia, and Rehnquist also demonstrate a considerable ideological slant in their voting patterns, as do Burger, O'Connor, and Kennedy to a somewhat lesser degree. Stewart and Powell appear least affected by ideology in that the probability with which they vote to invalidate conservative and liberal laws is about the same. The data presented in

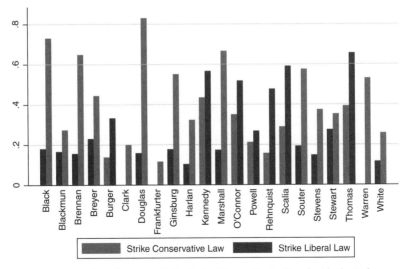

FIGURE 7 Proportion of Votes to Strike Federal Laws, Controlling for Ideological Direction of Substantive Policy

Figure 7 thus demonstrates the substantial role of ideology in decisions determining the constitutionality of federal legislation. A number of justices obviously show a significant disparity in the probabilities of their striking down a liberal as opposed to a conservative law, and vice versa.

The next step in measuring activism involves a more rigorous statistical analysis. In particular, we test whether ideology had a statistically significant influence on the justices' voting behavior. Moreover, because changes in the Court's agenda is a continuing concern when one compares justices across different time periods (particularly given the change in the governing juris-dictional statute noted above), we controlled for whether the lower court struck the statute at issue. While admittedly an imperfect measure of agenda control, the results nevertheless offer some measure of the Supreme Court's case selection processes as well as some control for the strength of the legal challenge presented. Thus for each justice, we estimated a logit model of their votes in cases raising challenges to federal enactments (coded 1 if they voted to strike the statute, and 0 otherwise), regressed on the statutory direc-tion of the substantive policy embodied in the statute (coded 1 for liberal statutes, 0 for neutral statutes, and -1 for conservative statutes) and the lower court's decision whether to strike (coded 1 if the lower court struck the stat-ute, and 0 otherwise). Based on these models, in Table 3 we present the prob-ability of a vote to invalidate a liberal, neutral, and conservative statute; the number of votes analyzed; and the p-value, which reflects whether the statu-tory ideology had a statistically significant impact on the justices' votes. P-values of less than .05 indicate such a significant relationship.

The results demonstrate a wide variation among the justices in their approach to the constitutionality of federal laws. As seen in Figure 7 as well, some justices, including White, Breyer, and Blackmun, were simply more def-erential to Congress overall, regardless of whether the statute was liberal or conservative. Not only is their probability of striking a statute fairly low, the statutory ideology variable does not reach conventional levels of statistical significance (although some are fairly close). Justice Blackmun's nonideologi-cal voting behavior may seem surprising, but this result may stem from his changing ideological orientation over time. His apparent neutrality may simply reflect his dramatic shift in voting behavior from conservative to liberal during his time on the Court.[54] Frankfurter and Harlan were also

---

54. The ideologies of justices sometimes change over time, a matter that has been well stud-ied by Lee Epstein and her coauthors Andrew Martin, Kevin Quinn, and Jeff Segal

TABLE 3 Probability of Justice Striking Federal Statute, Controlling for Lower Court Action

Justice	Probability Strike Liberal Statute	Probability Strike Neutral Statute	Probability Strike Conservative Statute	Number of Votes	P-Value (Ideology Variable)**
Black*	.181	.	.737	63	.000
Blackmun	.177	.209	.244	138	.427
Brennan*	.161	.374	.650	166	.000
Breyer	.208	.313	.442	55	.096
Burger	.426	.209	.086	108	.002
Clark*	.181	.	.731	40	.064
Douglas	.160	.	.830	84	.000
Frankfurter*	.000	.	.117	17	.343
Ginsburg	.159	.331	.565	59	.005
Harlan	.110	.	.305	56	.134
Kennedy	.695	.610	.517	80	.193
Marshall	.172	.409	.697	135	.000
O'Connor	.584	.446	.316	121	.016
Powell	.386	.244	.142	103	.041
Rehnquist	.519	.266	.109	188	.000
Scalia	.636	.453	.283	94	.003
Souter	.132	.362	.679	67	.002
Stevens	.141	.242	.381	163	.003
Stewart	.366	.	.318	114	.878
Thomas	.692	.552	.403	67	.030
Warren*	.000	.	.531	49	.000
White	.104	.156	.227	164	.077

Note: Missing values for neutral statutes exist because some of the justices did not consider cases challenging laws without a clear directional coding in the Spaeth Database.
* Justices' voting probabilities based on logit equation of statutory ideology or chi-square test due to co-linearity between independent and dependent variables.
** P-values of less than .05 reflect a statistically significant relationship between ideology and the justices' votes to strike federal laws.

deferential and relatively nonideological in their voting behavior, although the small number of cases for analysis means their results must be interpreted with caution. And while their voting behavior reflected some slight ideological bias, that ideological effect was not statistically significant, as

---

(Epstein et al. 2007). While such drift occurs among many justices, Blackmun's change was the most dramatic. He made a "near complete flip, from one of the Court's most conservative members to among its most consistent civil libertarians" (Epstein et al. 2007, 1494). Although Justice Blackmun argued that he didn't change as much as the Court itself changed, Justice Rehnquist served for a roughly similar period and did not show the same degree of change in decisional outcomes.

measured by the conventional .05 level. Justices Powell and Burger were also highly deferential in general, but when they did vote to strike, the evidence indicates that they did so more often in cases involving liberal statutes. And although he also voted to invalidate challenged statutes infrequently, Justice Stevens demonstrated an inclination to invalidate conservative laws more often than liberal laws.

Other justices were more activist in terms of their willingness to strike federal enactments, but did so in a relatively evenhanded manner. Justice Stewart, for example, had a probability of striking a statute between .316 and .366, but the difference between votes to strike liberal versus conservative statutes was not statistically significant. As with Stewart, Justice Kennedy's behavior was not significantly shaped by ideology, although he was some-what more inclined to strike liberal rather than conservative statutes. Nevertheless, he demonstrated a strong willingness to strike federal laws. Justice O'Connor was more deferential than Justice Kennedy on the whole, and showed a significantly greater inclination to strike liberal statutes, but the difference is not extreme, with a probability of striking a liberal statute at .584 and a conservative one at .316. Justice Stevens also shows a high level of deference to Congress but was more than twice as likely to strike a conserva-tive as to strike a liberal statute.

On the other hand, some justices were more clearly influenced by the ideological direction of the statute at issue. These included liberals such as Justices Douglas, Black, Marshall, Brennan, Souter, and Ginsburg, and con-servatives such as Justices Rehnquist, Scalia, and Thomas. Within this group, however, there are dramatic differences. Some justices were very deferential to statutes they favored ideologically. For example, liberal justices such as Marshall and Warren had a very low probability of voting to strike a liberal statute; Rehnquist and Burger had a very low probability of voting to strike a conservative statute. In contrast, Justice Scalia and, especially, Justice Thomas were relatively activist even in invalidating conservative statutes (though far more activist in the case of liberal statutes).

These results reveal the two distinct dimensions to judicial activism in this context. First, one might identify **institutional activism**, which reflects the justices' propensity to defer to the coordinate branches or to exercise judicial power to enforce the constitution, regardless of the ideology of the underlying statute. For federal laws, Justice Thomas clearly sits at the high end of this measure. Justice Thomas is quite willing to invalidate even con-servative federal enactments, but when those statutes are liberal, his voting behavior is the most aggressive among all the justices. Justice Kennedy is a close second by this measure. The other justices are substantially more deferential to congressional action.

The second dimension is **ideological activism**. This reflects a propensity to strike federal legislation that is contrary to the justice's ideology but a high propensity to uphold statutes that are ideologically aligned with the justice's preferences. This dimension is more common throughout the Court. From the Warren Court era, Justices Douglas, Brennan, and Marshall were very ideologically activist. More recently, this pattern is evident in the votes of Rehnquist and Scalia.

We categorize the justices based on these two dimensions, placing them in four groups, as set forth in Table 4. The category "high institutional/high ideological activism" describes justices who are strongly influenced by their ideology and who are not particularly deferential to Congress. The category "high institutional/low ideological activism" describes justices who show a willingness to strike congressional enactments but who also do not demonstrate significant ideological voting patterns. Only Kennedy fits in this category. The category "low institutional/high ideological activism" includes justices who defer to Congress but who are ideological in their votes. The final category of "low institutional/low ideological activism" reflects justices who are deferential to Congress and who are also nonideological in their voting behavior.

TABLE 4 Taxonomy of Judicial Behavior—Votes to Invalidate Federal Enactments

Institutional Activism	Ideological Activism	
	High	Low
High	Marshall	Kennedy
	Brennan	
	Thomas	
	Scalia	
	Souter	
	O'Connor	
	Douglas	
	Black	
Low	Burger	Blackmun
	Rehnquist	Breyer
	Ginsburg	White
	Stevens	Powell
	Clark	Stewart
	Warren	Frankfurter
		Harlan

The results generally conform to popular impressions of the justices, though some results may be surprising. Justice O'Connor is not generally characterized as a strong conservative, though she was fairly ideological in these cases. Readers might be surprised to see Justice Blackmun in the most restraintist category, but they should bear in mind that this analysis considers only federal laws and evaluates his entire career. The depiction of Justice Kennedy as a nonideological activist fits his general profile. Similarly, we suspect most observers would list Justices White, Powell, Stewart, and Breyer as among the more deferential justices for this time period.

The meaning of the various categories is not determinate if one is seeking the "most activist justice." Obviously, the justices in the "high institutional/ high ideological activism" category are likely candidates for most activist under the term's conventional meaning. One might argue, however, that the "high institutional/low ideological activism" category may reflect the true legal activist, aggressively invalidating both liberal and conservative laws. Indeed, Justice Kennedy had the highest rate for voting to strike neutral laws of any of our surveyed justices.

⑉ D. Conclusion

The Court's invalidation of a federal statute is often presented as the paradigmatic case of judicial activism, and is used by many as the single measure of such activism. This position centrally reflects the counter-majoritarian criticism of judicial activism, as well as other theories related to the separation of powers. By this measure, the most activist justices were Warren Court liberals and some contemporary justices, including conservatives such as Thomas and Scalia. Ideological moderates tend to be less activist, though Justice Kennedy stands out as not particularly deferential to Congress but relatively nonideological as well.

Of course, this chapter only considered decisions invalidating federal laws. While such decisions are often regarded as the archetype of judicial activism, they are not the only instances of activism. In terms of absolute numbers, the Court has been less likely to strike down federal laws than other government actions, such as the laws of state and local governments, which we analyze in the next chapter.

FOUR

Judicial Review of State and Local Laws

IN THIS CHAPTER, we turn our attention to the Court's review of the actions of democratically elected state and local governments. Like invalidations of federal laws, the Court's decision to invalidate state or even local enactments implicates counter-majoritarian concerns—at least within the confines of the particular jurisdiction. Here we consider the frequency with which the justices voted to invalidate state and local laws throughout the Warren, Burger, and Rehnquist Courts. Like our measure of activism in the federal context, we focus on two dimensions of activism in the state context. First, we measure how often the individual justices voted to invalidate state or local laws. Second, we consider whether those votes were driven by the justices' personal policy preferences.

✼ A. The Standard: Declaring State Laws Unconstitutional

A number of scholars, judges, and commentators have considered the import of the exercise of judicial review by federal courts over state legislation, with most believing that invalidation of state laws is less consequential (and thus less "activist") than the invalidation of federal enactments. For example, Bradley Canon characterizes the former as highly activist but the latter as only "somewhat activist" (Canon 1984, 405). This perspective is often based, in part, on the fact that federal enactments emerge from the coordinate branches of the federal government. As a consequence, their invalidation constitutes a more dramatic "rebuke" to institutions coequal in stature to the Court itself. As Judge Easterbrook has argued, it is "more presumptuous for tenured federal officials to upset decisions of the political branches of the national government, than it is for the national government (of which judges are just agents) to impose its will on the states" (Easterbrook 2002, 1404). Moreover, by invalidating federal legislation, the Court risks retaliation from

Congress in the form of jurisdictional limitations, budgetary constraints, or even reversal (Handberg and Hill 1980, Meernik and Ignagni 1997). The same retaliation is possible when the Court strikes down state legislation, but the direct challenge to congressional authority is not present. It might thus be said that the Court takes greater institutional risks when it invalidates a federal rather than a state enactment.

The notion that the invalidation of state statutes is relatively less activist also rests on constitutional grounds. Certainly, the Constitution's Supremacy Clause bolsters such a view: as Oliver Wendell Holmes suggested, while the United States would not "come to an end" if the Court lost its power to invalidate federal statutes, it would be "imperiled" if the Court lost its power to invalidate state laws (Holmes 1920, 295–296). Section 1 of the Fourteenth Amendment, which imposes equal protection and due process limitations on state governments, further supports this view (Zietlow 2008, 274). These constitutional provisions clearly delineate federal authority over the states, and judicial review provides the means to enforce this balance of power.

Yet while the constitutional structure supports the federal government's hegemony over the states in various ways, striking state statutes may have substantial national policy significance. First, the invalidation of a state law may, by implication, invalidate comparable policies in numerous other states. In addition, the decision may influence future policy choices made by all state governments, as well as by the federal government itself. The decision in _Roe v. Wade_[55] striking a state antiabortion law obviously shaped the choices available to state and even federal legislators interested in curtailing abortion rights. Such decisions may have a substantial chilling effect on a state's willingness to experiment in a particular policy area (Hoekstra 2005). The effect of invalidating state legislation is not limited to the particular law at issue, therefore, but also extends to policy initiatives that are foregone or passed in modified form because of the Court's decision.

As for counter-majoritarianism, one might also argue that the Court's invalidation of a state law is less activist because it does not necessarily invalidate a policy favored by the national electorate. Indeed, to the extent the Court's decision conforms to the public mood at the national level, its decision arguably constitutes a majoritarian, rather than counter-majoritarian act. Scot Powe makes this argument with respect to Warren Court activism, which he suggests served to impose a national majority's view on the

---

55. 410 U.S. 113 (1973).

contrary views of a state or region (Powe 2000). The Court was therefore favoring the policy goals of a national majority over those of a localized majority.

On the other hand, this distinction begs the question regarding the relevant majority for consideration. The United States federal system of government protects states' sovereignty and authority to legislate in particular areas so as to further the preferences of the state's popular electorate, even if those preferences are contrary to those of the national majority. Embodied in this perspective is the idea that the states provide the nation with "laboratories of democracy," as Justice Brandeis famously described them, that enable policy experimentation within confined geographic spheres.[56] Furthermore, as Jonathan Casper has noted, "it is . . . difficult to make the determination of the preferences of the national majority" on issues involving individual state laws (Casper 1976, 59). Even assuming that the Court did understand the national will on a policy implicated by a particular state law provision, Congress itself often has the authority to override state legislation with a federal statute that preempts contrary state laws under the Constitution's Supremacy Clause. If Congress has the authority to act under the Commerce Clause or some other constitutional provision, its failure to enact such a preemptive statute might be considered a national determination to leave the matter to state choice, in which case the Supreme Court's invalidation of a state law would be contrary to that majoritarian preference. Even where Congress does not have constitutional authority to act, it can often force the issue by means of grant-in-aid programs or other funding devices that enable the federal government to regulate state action "with a velvet glove."[57]

One might even argue that the constitutional review of state statutes enables greater activism than review of federal legislation. Pursuant to doctrines of justiciability, the Supreme Court is limited to rendering opinions in cases with live disputes. Nevertheless, the Court receives thousands of petitions each year from which to form its docket. A Court interested in promoting its own policy preferences would seek to formulate the broadest portfolio

---

56. *New State Ice Co. v. Liebmann,* 285 U.S. 262, 311 (1932) (Brandeis, J., dissenting) ("[I]t is one of the happy accidents of the federal system that a single courageous state may, if its citizens choose, serve as a laboratory, and try novel social and economic experiments without risk to the rest of the country.").

57. Indeed, with the exception of the Unfunded Mandates Reform Act of 1995, Congress has made little progress of late in enacting legislation that otherwise protects state interests from federal interference (Dinan 2004).

of policy issues available. With their diverse circumstances and preferences, the enactments of the 50 states are likely to present many more constitutional questions than the single federal government. Thus the civil rights activism of the *Brown* era was primarily enabled by state actions compelling segregation. Similarly, there was no federal law comparable to the Connecticut statute struck in *Griswold*,[58] but via *Griswold* the Court was able to create a constitutional protection for personal privacy.

This thesis seems to find support in evidence concerning the precedential impact of court decisions. While the policy significance of individual decisions is difficult to measure, the importance of a case as precedential authority has been measured through sophisticated techniques of network analysis using the frequency of citations in later Supreme Court opinions. A recent study found that the most important case according to this measure is *Cantwell v. Connecticut*,[59] in which the Court struck down a state statute restricting freedom of religion (Fowler et al. 2007). The second most important case in the network was *Schneider v. State of New Jersey*,[60] which invalidated local regulations limiting the distribution of handbills, as restrictive of free speech. Indeed, *all* of the 15 most important precedents involved the Court's review of state or local government action. The most significant case reviewing any federal action was ranked sixteenth (*Roth v. United States*[61]). Yet even *Roth* was combined with review of a state action and *upheld* the federal prosecution as constitutional. At least by this standard of precedential importance, judicial review of state action appears no less activist than review of federal action.

One might argue for a very different reason that the invalidation of state legislation is *more* activist than striking federal legislation. A key purpose of the original Constitution was to constrain the power of the *federal* government. While the Fourteenth Amendment and the Court's subsequent application of the Bill of Rights to state governments certainly altered this focus (Berger 1977), the concern about excessive exercise of federal powers persists. The Articles of the Constitution provide limited legislative authority to the federal government and set forth specific restrictions on the exercise of those limited powers. The Constitution also protects certain principles

---

58. 381 U.S. 479 (1965).

59. 310 U.S. 296 (1940).

60. 308 U.S. 147 (1939).

61. 354 U.S. 476 (1957).

associated with federalism and the separation of powers. Given these critical elements of the Constitution constraining legislative action and preserving a federal system of separated powers, invalidation of a federal statute infringing on these principles appears well within the Court's purview. In contrast, the invalidation of a state statute does little to contribute to these particular goals.

Moreover, striking a federal statute on structural federalism grounds may not necessarily carry much in the way of policy costs. A ruling that the federal government lacks the authority to adopt a particular statute in no way prevents the states from enacting identical legislation with the same effect, albeit implemented by a different government. In *United States v. Lopez*,[62] for example, the Court struck down a federal law prohibiting guns within a school zone as beyond the scope of the government's Commerce Clause authority. Although this ruling constrained Congress from acting further to limit gun possession near schools, *Lopez* did not create a policy vacuum because many states and school districts already had similar restrictions and the rest retained the power to enact their own. As a result, "*Lopez* resulted in very little change in substantive law" in the United States (Kerr 2003, 31). That is not to say that *Lopez* did not have a chilling effect on congressional action in other areas; it well might have had such an effect. But the point remains that striking federal legislation does not inevitably have broader policy implications than striking state legislation.

One additional factor raises particular concerns about invalidation of state legislation. The justices of the Supreme Court are, of course, employees of the federal government, from which they receive salaries and other resources and upon which they are dependent for enforcement of judicial orders. Lacking the purse or the sword, the justices may be concerned that invalidation of federal legislation might produce legislative initiatives to curtail the Court's power or resources. In her 1991 study of congressional influence over the Court by means of budgetary constraints, for example, Eugenia Toma found that Congress signals its disapproval of Court decisions by manipulating the size of the Court's budget and that the Court "responds to the budgetary signals by altering its decisions in the direction desired by Congress" (Toma 1991, 145). Other mechanisms also provide Congress with leverage over a disfavored Court, including jurisdiction-stripping legislation, a refusal to fill lower court vacancies, or even impeachment (Toma, 133). One might therefore expect the justices to place a "thumb on the scale" in

---

62. 514 U.S. 549 (1995).

favor of the federal government when reviewing federal action but be far less deferential when reviewing the actions of state governments. Indeed, some have argued that the historical record supports the view that the Supreme Court has promoted the centralization of government in the United States (Shapiro 1981, 28). For example, Philip Kurland has suggested that the "Supreme Court has persistently and consistently acted as a centripetal force favoring, at almost every chance, the national authority over that of the states" (Kurland 1978, 156–157).

But we need not take a final position on the normative debate over the relative significance of striking state and federal laws. Rather, we simply note that there are reasonable arguments suggesting that striking a state statute may constitute a highly consequential act, both legally and practically. From any standpoint in the analysis of activism, it is hard to avoid the fact that the most controversial Supreme Court cases, ranging from *Brown* to *Roe*, have involved state legislation. For these reasons, invalidation of state laws, even though they do not necessarily challenge an expression of the national majority's will, represents a critical dimension within the multidimensional concept of judicial activism.

ⅷ B. Invalidations over Time

As was the case with our review of the Court's invalidation of federal statutes, we begin with analysis of the average annual frequency with which the Court invalidated state statutes on constitutional grounds, using data provided by the Congressional Research Service. As in Chapter 3, we categorized the Courts of the twentieth century by Chief Justice, except that the post-"switch in time that saved nine" Court is referred to as the Roosevelt Court (1937 to 1953). For the Courts with long tenure, we separated the Early Warren Court (1954–1962) from the Late Warren Court (1963–1969), and the Early Rehnquist Court (1986–1994) from the Late Rehnquist Court (1995–2004. Figure 8 presents the number of decisions striking state laws for the different Court periods; we included the average number of federal invalidations for purposes of comparison.

These data conform reasonably well to the conventional wisdom regarding the Court's exercise of judicial review throughout the various eras. The later Warren and Burger Courts invalidated state statutes with the greatest frequency, a trend that saw a significant decline under Chief Justice Rehnquist. And the high rates of the White and Taft Courts should not be overlooked. In contrast, the Roosevelt Court appears quite restraintist, an unsurprising fact given the switch in time in the 1930s that produced greater support for

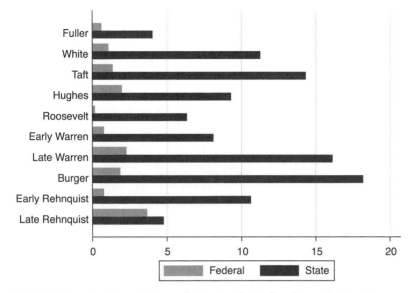

FIGURE 8 Mean Yearly Invalidations of Federal and State/Local Laws, by Court Era

federal legislation addressing the economic crisis. With respect to the comparison between state and federal enactments, every era saw the Court invalidating more state statutes on average than federal laws. The ratio of state to federal invalidations, however, varied considerably over time and ultimately reached near equality in the Late Rehnquist Court. Indeed, the Late Rehnquist Court is unique, as every other era saw the Court striking state statutes at a much higher frequency, on average, per term. In a descriptive sense, these results suggest that the Rehnquist Court seemed unusually activist with respect to striking federal laws and unusually restraintist with respect to state laws. In general, however, the explanation for the disparity between state and federal invalidations may have more to do with opportunity than with inclination: at least during the Warren and Burger Courts, the justices were presented with many more challenges to state laws than to federal enactments, no doubt due to the plethora of legislation produced by the state governments as well as to those Courts' propensities toward expanding the Supreme Court docket by selecting more cases for review.

Figure 9 presents data on the frequency of challenges to and invalidations of state statutes per term on the Warren, Burger, and Rehnquist Courts.[63]

63. The frequencies in Figure 9 do not perfectly track those in Figure 8 because the Congressional Research Service includes summary affirmances in its data; we include only those decisions decided with oral argument or with a written opinion (signed or per curiam).

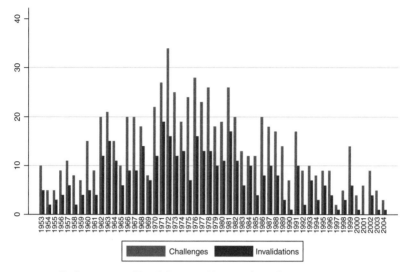

FIGURE 9 Challenges to and Invalidations of State and Local Laws, per Court Term

The most notable pattern is the burst of activity in this area during the Burger Court; that Court reviewed many more challenges and ultimately invalidated more state statutes than either the Warren or the Rehnquist Courts. In part, this pattern is due simply to the Burger Court's expansive docket. Relative to its predecessor Courts, the Burger Court's plenary docket grew substantially after 1971, a fact that is reflected in the data presented in Figure 9. Compared with the Warren Court, which decided on average about 110 cases per term, the Burger Court's docket ultimately mushroomed to 175 cases per year on average (O'Brien 2005).

It is also possible that the comparative frequency with which the Burger Court reviewed the constitutionality of state laws is due, in part, to a federal statute that granted a right to direct appeal to the Supreme Court from any circuit court judgment invalidating a state statute on constitutional grounds. Congress repealed this mandatory jurisdiction in 1988. We noted in Chapter 3, however, that the impact of this preexisting right to direct appeal should probably not be overestimated. As Arthur Hellman observed in his evaluations of the Rehnquist Court's shrinking docket, "[T]he elimination of mandatory jurisdiction played no more than a minuscule role in the shrinkage of the plenary docket in the 1990s" (Hellman 1996, 412).[64] Moreover, since

64. Professor Hellman explained in 1985 why the Court's mandatory jurisdiction actually had less effect than one might expect on its plenary docket: "[i]n recent Terms most appeals

that law was in place during the Warren Court as well, it is unlikely it alone accounts for the obvious increase in activity in this area in the 1970s and early 1980s. Rather, the likely explanation for the changes over time involve the number of cases available for review, as well as, in the later period, the Rehnquist Court justices' view that the role of the Court in the American legal system should be limited (Hellman 1996, 430).

Interestingly, although one often associates the Warren Court with an aggressive approach to judicial review of state enactments, in fact the Warren Court as a whole invalidated state statutes less frequently than did the Burger Court. For cases decided on the plenary docket (with argument and opinion, and thus excluding summary affirmances and reversals), the Warren Court invalidated almost 7 state or local laws each term, the Burger Court about 11.5, and the Rehnquist Court only about 4. As far as the *rate* at which each Court invalidated statutes once a challenge was brought, however, the Warren and Burger Courts acted in a remarkably similar fashion. Of cases granted plenary review, the Warren Court invalidated about 54% of state statutes challenged before it, the Burger Court about 55%. In contrast, the Rehnquist Court *upheld* almost 58% of all state or local laws challenged on constitutional grounds. To the extent the Rehnquist Court was more predisposed to protect state legislative prerogatives in the interests of federalism, its actions were consistent with that predisposition—at least when compared with the Rehnquist Court's two predecessor Courts.

Comparison of the three Courts' activity in this area therefore suggests that while the Warren Court is most often associated with activism in the form of invalidation of state laws, the true prize must go to the Burger Court. Although the Warren and Burger Courts invalidated at about the same *rate*, the latter invalidated *more frequently*. This finding is consistent with the idea, expressed in Chapter 1, that Nixon's appointees did little to rein in activism on the Supreme Court. Moreover, it is also possible that the precedents rendered by the Warren Court, establishing as they did more expansive civil liberties claims, laid the foundation for future litigants to bring constitutional challenges in federal court and win on appeal before the Supreme Court. In explaining why the Burger Court did not fully retrench the Warren Court's

---

have been disposed of by summary unexplicated orders affirming the judgment of the court below. In appeals from federal courts, the disposition is one of affirmance eo nomine; appeals from state courts are dismissed 'for want of a substantial federal question'" (Hellman 1985, 953).

civil libertarianism, Larry Baum has suggested that the Warren Court's expansive precedents in the area of civil liberties

> helped to shape the Court's agenda. By the late 1960s a high proportion of the cases brought to the Court involved civil liberties claims—in part because of the Warren Court's implicit encouragement. And the private interest groups most skilled at getting strong cases to the Court, such as the NAACP and the American Civil Liberties Union, were devoted to these kinds of claims. While the Court simply could have refused to hear all these cases, many were sufficiently attractive to the required four justices to gain full hearings (Baum 1987, 25).

Thus the Burger Court continued the Warren Court revolution by addressing the burst in litigation that followed the Warren Court's establishment or reinvigoration of causes of action protecting individual rights. And of course it was the Burger Court that produced decisions invalidating state statutes on grounds that they violated women's rights to equal protection under the Fourteenth Amendment, required desegregation outside the Southern states, or allowed arbitrary application of the death penalty. These new doctrinal developments resulted in the Burger Court's striking more than 200 laws, "an unprecedented number," even as compared with the Warren Court (Baum 1987, 22).

❧ C. The Voting Behavior of the Individual Justices

Having compared the Supreme Court's general propensity to invalidate state statutes over time, we now turn our attention to the individual justices' votes in these cases. Several scholars have analyzed the justices' voting behavior in cases challenging state and local legislation before the Court. In her comprehensive study of the natural Rehnquist Court[65] between 1994 and 2004, Lori Ringhand analyzed the justices' votes on the constitutionality of state statutes challenged during that period and reviewed by the Court (Ringhand 2007). Her analysis revealed a very different pattern in state cases than was found in cases raising challenges to federal statutes. The more liberal justices,

---

65. As noted previously, a "natural court" describes a Court whose membership does not change during the relevant period.

such as Stevens and Souter, were more likely to strike a state law than were conservatives such as Justices Rehnquist, Thomas, and Scalia. In contrast, conservative justices during that period were more likely to vote to strike federal legislation. This pattern was also evident in work by Solberg and Lindquist (2007), which found that liberals on the Rehnquist Court were more likely than conservatives to vote to strike state or local legislation.

Both studies, however, also found that the justices' willingness to strike state laws appeared to hinge substantially on the substantive policies embodied in the challenged legislation. Although this pattern was somewhat more pronounced for liberal than for conservative justices, both groups were more likely to vote to uphold statutes that conformed to their ideological preferences. Howard and Segal (2004) came to similar conclusions in their study of the justices' voting behavior in cases challenging state and federal legislation over the period from 1985 to 1994. They concluded that "[c]learly, ideological considerations predominate in the decision to strike legislation" (Howard and Segal 2004, 138). In his earlier study of the Court's activity in this area between 1837 and 1964, John Gates reached the same conclusion. In his assessment of the Warren Court, Gates observed that "the Court was prone to invalidate state policies . . . enacted by state governments whose partisan or ideological orientation was opposed to the dominant majority on the Court" (Gates 1987, 275).

1. The Frequency of the Justices' Votes to Strike State and Local Legislation

As in Chapter 3, we relied on the U.S. Supreme Court Database to compile data on the individual justices' votes in cases challenging state or local legislation during the Warren, Burger, and Rehnquist Courts. Our data include cases in which a statute was challenged and invalidated, as well as those in which the statute was challenged but upheld. Figure 10 and Table 5 present data on the mean number of votes each justice cast per term to strike state or local legislation for the period that justice served on the Court. Table 5 provides information about the number of votes used to calculate this statistic; Figure 10 sets forth these data graphically so that the magnitude of the justices' behavior may be compared more easily.

Not surprisingly, justices who served for long periods on the Burger Court rank high on this measure. Even Justices Stewart and Powell, not known for being particularly activist justices, have a high mean frequency of votes to

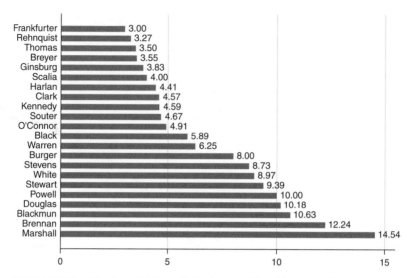

FIGURE 10 Mean Number of Votes to Strike State and Local Laws, per Court Term

TABLE 5 Mean Votes to Strike State and Local Laws per Court Term

Justice	Mean Votes to Strike	Number of Votes	Court Terms
Black	5.89	225	1953–1970
Blackmun	10.63	448	1970–1993
Brennan	12.24	591	1956–1989
Breyer	3.55	74	1994–2004
Burger	8.00	348	1969–1985
Clark	4.57	159	1953–1966
Douglas	10.18	325	1953–1975
Frankfurter	3.00	74	1953–1961
Ginsburg	3.83	84	1993–2004
Harlan	4.41	210	1954–1970
Kennedy	4.59	161	1987–2004
Marshall	14.54	457	1967–1990
O'Connor	4.91	265	1981–2004
Powell	10.00	314	1971–1986
Rehnquist	3.27	478	1971–2004
Scalia	4.00	185	1986–2004
Souter	4.67	115	1990–2004
Stevens	8.73	387	1975–2004
Stewart	9.39	425	1958–1980
Thomas	3.50	106	1991–2004
Warren	6.25	193	1953–1968
White	8.97	578	1961–1992

strike during their tenure on the Court. The most activist justices are liberals Marshall and Brennan, who served under all three chief justices. During their lengthy tenures, the two voted to strike state laws more often per term than any other justice over the period from 1953 to 2004. More contemporary liberals, such as Justices Souter, Ginsburg, and Breyer, voted far less often to strike state statutes, but again, this is the likely result of their service on the Court during a period of dramatic docket contraction. Conservatives, especially Justices Rehnquist and Thomas, appear much more deferential. And although he served only until 1961, Frankfurter's behavior is consistent with his reputation as a justice committed to judicial restraint.

We also calculated the probability that a justice would vote to strike a state law once a challenge was brought before the Court; these probabilities are presented in Figure 11. In effect, this approach allows us to control for the opportunity to strike state statutes and thus compare somewhat more effectively across Court eras. In cases granted plenary review, we see that, once again, Justices Marshall and Brennan are most likely to vote to invalidate state or local legislation once the opportunity is presented to them. And by this measure, current liberal appointees to the Court appear more activist, with Souter, Ginsburg, and Breyer voting to strike state legislation more than half the time. Among the conservative justices, Rehnquist leads in restraint-oriented behavior, voting to strike state or local legislation only about 20% of

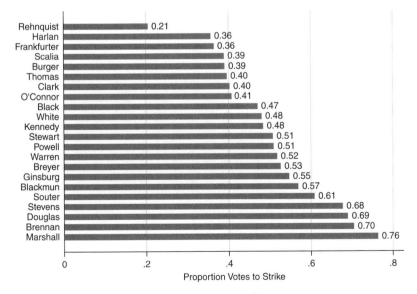

FIGURE 11 Probability of Vote to Strike State or Local Law

the time. The scores closest to Rehnquist's—those of Frankfurter and Harlan—exceed Rehnquist's score by 15%. Three more conservatives, Scalia, Burger, and Thomas, are close behind, voting to invalidate in about 40% of the challenges presented to them for review.

2. The Voting Behavior of the Individual Justices as Influenced by Ideology

As we argued in Chapter 3, frequencies and probabilities of votes to invalidate are incomplete; to paint a complete portrait of activist behavior, judicial ideology must also be taken into account. We begin that enterprise by presenting the probabilities that each justice voted to strike or uphold state statutes, controlling for the ideological direction of the statutory policy at issue. As in Chapter 3, we coded a statute's substantive policy direction using the directionality codes included in the U.S. Supreme Court Database. Where the statute was struck and the outcome of the case was coded liberal, we coded the statute as embodying a conservative policy, and vice versa. Figure 12 presents these results graphically, with the proportion of votes to strike conservative laws reflected in the height of the left bar for each justice, and the proportion of votes to strike liberal laws in the bar on the right.

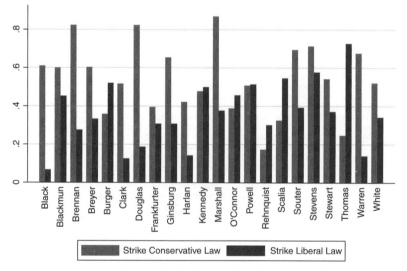

FIGURE 12 Proportion of Votes to Strike State and Local Laws, Controlling for Ideological Direction of Substantive Policy

These data demonstrate that, for some justices, ideology played an important role in their decisions regarding the constitutionality of state or local legislation. Liberals Black, Brennan, Douglas, Marshall, and Warren show a pronounced difference in their propensity to strike liberal as opposed to conservative laws. To a somewhat lesser degree, the same can be said for Justices Breyer, Ginsburg, Souter, and Clark. Among the conservatives, Justice Thomas shows the greatest degree of ideological disparity in voting behavior, with a proportion of votes to strike liberal laws more than twice the proportion of votes to strike conservative statutes. Justices Burger, Scalia, and Rehnquist show similar tendencies, but their ideological voting pattern is not as pronounced as that of Justice Thomas. Other justices are remarkably even-handed in their approach to judicial review of state legislation. Justices Blackmun, Frankfurter, Stevens, Kennedy, O'Connor, Powell, and Stewart show no substantial preference for either liberal or conservative polices. In the case of Blackmun and Stevens, however, these data could mask differences in their voting behavior over time. Blackmun, in particular, is known for his considerable shift in ideological voting behavior during his long tenure on the Court (Greenhouse 2006); the same is likely true for Stevens as well. Indeed, after 1985, Stevens voted to strike conservative state statutes 75% of the time, but voted to strike only 45% of the time when a liberal statute was challenged. Similarly, after 1985, Blackmun voted to strike conservative statutes 75% of the time, but only in about 37% of cases in which a liberal statute was challenged.

To conduct a more rigorous statistical test of the ideological differences across the justices' voting behavior in these cases, we calculated the probability that each justice would vote to overturn a state or local law based on that law's ideological direction, controlling for whether the lower court voted to strike the law. As we noted in Chapter 3, this test enables us to include a rough control for the Court's agenda setting process and for the relative strength of the arguments in favor of striking or upholding the law. The probabilities that each justice would vote to strike a liberal or conservative statute, as well as the statistical significance of the ideology variable, are set forth in Table 6.[66] P-values of less than .05 indicate that ideology is significantly related to the justices' voting behavior.

---

66. Unlike in the federal cases, none of the state and local statutes reviewed were characterized as ideologically neutral.

TABLE 6 Probability of Justice Striking State Statute, Controlling for Lower Court Action

Justice	Probability Strike Liberal Statute	Probability Strike Conservative Statute	Number of Votes	P-Value (Ideology Variable)*
Black	.073	.609	225	.000
Blackmun	.550	.619	448	.236
Brennan	.356	.857	591	.000
Breyer	.352	.602	74	.063
Burger	.563	.343	348	.001
Clark	.150	.517	159	.000
Douglas	.213	.841	325	.000
Frankfurter	.321	.386	74	.587
Ginsburg	.350	.661	84	.014
Harlan	.145	.420	210	.001
Kennedy	.614	.479	161	.157
Marshall	.450	.886	457	.000
O'Connor	.513	.365	265	.043
Powell	.609	.512	314	.168
Rehnquist	.342	.150	478	.000
Scalia	.616	.287	185	.000
Souter	.450	.704	115	.016
Stevens	.618	.712	387	.082
Stewart	.417	.545	425	.043
Thomas	.747	.233	106	.000
Warren	.150	.674	193	.000
White	.377	.515	578	.009

* P-values of less than .05 reflect a statistically significant relationship between ideology and the justices votes to strike federal laws

Once again, most of the justices show significant ideological skewing in the outcome of their votes. In general, the probability of striking a state law is higher than the probability of striking a federal statute, but we continue to see disparities among the justices that are similar to those found in the preceding chapter. Some justices show a significantly greater willingness to strike one type of statute than the other, and are relatively deferential to statutes that conform to their ideological preferences. Others are more activist across the board. As revealed in Figure 12, in several instances the justices' policy preferences appeared to have little impact on their decisions to strike state and local legislation. In particular, the p-values for the equations reflecting the voting behavior of Justices Blackmun, Powell, Stevens, Breyer, Kennedy, and Frankfurter do not achieve conventional levels of statistical significance in a two-tailed test, although several are close. In the cases of Blackmun and Stevens, this result likely masks greater ideological voting at the end of their careers, but in terms of overall career scores, these justices are fairly evenhanded in their willingness to strike liberal and conservative legislation. Other justices demonstrate a low probability of voting to strike regardless of the ideological direction of the statute at issue: Rehnquist clearly falls into this category, as does Harlan, Clark, Frankfurter, and White to a lesser degree. Most willing to strike statutes based on ideology are Marshall, Brennan, Douglas, Thomas, Black, and Warren.

As in the preceding chapter, based on the statistics presented in Table 6, we categorized the justices into four groups based on two distinct dimensions of judicial activism: **institutional activism** and **ideological activism**. Justices are coded as institutionally activist if they demonstrate a fairly high probability overall of striking state statutes. They are coded as ideologically activist if their decisions to strike are significantly affected by the ideological direction of the statute at issue, with large actual differences in their propensity to strike liberal as opposed to conservative statutes. Table 7 displays our assessments of the justices on activism in the context of state law invalidation.

As compared with the analysis of federal statutes, the results show some obvious commonalities and some obvious differences. Again, the "low institutional/high ideological activism" category includes Justices Marshall,

TABLE 7 Taxonomy of Judicial Behavior—Votes to Invalidate State and Local Legislation

Institutional Activism	Ideological Activism	
	High	Low
High	Marshall	Powell
	Brennan	Blackmun
	Thomas	Stevens
	Warren	Stewart
	Douglas	Kennedy
	Black	Breyer
	Souter	
Low	Rehnquist	Frankfurter
	Harlan	O'Connor
	Scalia	White
	Ginsburg	
	Burger	
	Clark	

Brennan, Thomas, Douglas, and Black. However, Justice Scalia moved to "low institutional/high ideological" and Justice O'Connor to "low institutional/low ideological," although this latter characterization is a close call. Although we categorized only one justice as exhibiting high institutional activism and low ideological activism in the federal context, here we see a number of justices who are quite willing to strike state statutes but do so without a significant or strong ideological valence. In this category, Kennedy is now joined by Powell, Blackmun, Stevens, Breyer, and Stewart. Our placement is somewhat subjective, however. While Justice White showed a statistically significant ideological pattern to his voting behavior, the ratio of his ideological voting was materially less than for the other high ideological justices, so we placed him in the low ideological sector. We drew a similar conclusion for Justice O'Connor.

We conclude with one point of caution regarding our results. As we noted earlier, these scores and categories reflect the justices' career scores, covering different periods on the Court. Had Souter or Ginsburg served on the Warren Court, their scores with respect to ideological deference might be quite low, since that Court considered different—and perhaps more patently unconstitutional—state legislation. Justice Harlan might provide another example. Although his reputation is not particularly liberal, Justice Harlan voted to strike conservative laws more often than liberal ones during his service on the Warren Court. This result could simply be a function of the types and qualities of the laws reviewed by that Court. And we have already noted that career scores may mask significant changes in voting behavior over a justice's entire career. These problems are inherent to some degree when comparing across Courts and justices. Nevertheless, despite their dependence on the Court's agenda, the statistics presented in this chapter reveal that the justices vary substantially in their treatment and approach to the constitutionality of state legislation.

✹ D. Conclusion

Including the invalidation of state laws in analyses of activism is important, but it is sometimes overlooked in assessments that focus primarily on federal legislation. The Court more frequently reviews challenges to the constitutionality of state laws than to federal law; thus its invalidation of state laws is more common. Our analysis reveals some rough similarity in the justices' approaches to federal and state legislation, but the justices on average show greater overall activism when reviewing state laws. Even if one accepts the debatable conclusion that striking an individual state law is less significant than striking a single federal law, the higher rate of activism in state law actions shows that these cases must be considered. And as with federal laws, the influence of ideology in these state cases remains profound for some, but not all, of the justices in our sample.

FIVE

Judicial Review of Executive Branch Actions

IN THE PRECEDING CHAPTERS, we analyzed the justices' treatment of cases challenging the constitutionality of legislation. Because popular elections make legislators directly accountable to the people, this dimension is often cited as the most critical measure of judicial activism. On the other hand, legislators are not the only elected officials in American government who represent majority preferences: presidents and governors are also elected and their actions may thus be presumed to reflect the popular will.

Chief executives often must act through an existing bureaucracy when implementing governmental policies, however, and agency heads are typically appointed rather than elected. At the lower echelons in most bureaucracies, employees are protected by civil service laws such that they are not subject to direct control by the president or governor. As a consequence, administrative agencies are seldom viewed as institutions that make policy in accordance with the majority will.[67] This perspective is further promoted by the notion that bureaucrats are neutral experts appointed for their technical expertise rather than their policy preferences. Judicial review of administrative action may therefore seem less likely to elicit charges of judicial activism, especially to the extent that charges of activism focus on judges' improper intrusion into the democratic process.

Yet bureaucracies are subject to extensive oversight and control by both the legislative branch and the chief executive, and a growing body of social scientific evidence suggests that administrative officials at all levels are often quite responsive to their political principals. For these reasons, judicial invalidation of agency decision making has the potential to produce counter-majoritarian results, albeit in a slightly different form than invalidation of

---

67. A large literature has developed around the idea that bureaucracies may be made more representative and responsive to the electorate if they are characterized by a diverse workforce (Meier, Wrinkle, and Polinard 1999).

legislative action. At the very least, aggressive judicial review may result in judges imposing their own policy preferences on the executive branch. Such infringement on the prerogatives of a coordinate branch is often cited as the hallmark of judicial activism. Judicial review of administrative policy making thus constitutes a fitting addition to our multidimensional conception of judicial activism.

In this chapter, we assess the manner in which the Court has reviewed the actions of officials in the executive branch, focusing on actions taken by federal regulatory or administrative social agencies.[68] In our empirical analysis, we first consider the frequency with which the justices voted to strike administrative action by the federal government throughout the Warren, Burger, and Rehnquist Courts. We also distinguish between judicial review of independent regulatory commissions, which are arguably subject to less presidential control, and executive branch agencies, which are governed by agency heads directly answerable to the president. We then turn to analyze the extent to which the justices' votes to review executive action are shaped by their ideological predispositions, as we continue to investigate the idea that activism is best measured in terms of result-oriented judging.

We add one preliminary caveat: although judicial invalidations of law enforcement action often give rise to charges of activism (consider *Miranda v. Arizona*,[69] for example), we do not evaluate the justices' voting behavior in cases involving criminal rights. First, to the extent they involve prevailing statutes that undermine defendants' rights, some of those cases are already included in our analyses in Chapters 3 and 4. Second, they are essentially impossible to analyze as a singular group using our measures of ideology because every decision invalidating an unlawful search and seizure, for example, is considered liberal in the U.S. Supreme Court Judicial Database. Thus our measures of activism (frequency of invalidation and result-oriented judging) would be perfectly collinear: votes to invalidate would always be liberal and vice versa. This situation provides us with no purchase on the question whether a justice's decision to invalidate is driven by the underlying substantive policy judgment at issue. Nevertheless, we have ample data to evaluate other forms of action taken by administrative agencies in other

---

68. Although the Supreme Court does occasionally review the actions of state agencies for constitutional violations, the frequency of such review is far less than for review of federal action. For that reason, we focus on judicial review of federal administrative action in this chapter.

69. 384 U.S. 436 (1966).

contexts, and in those contexts we do not encounter the same problem of collinearity. Some administrative agency decisions produce conservative substantive results (drawing back on environmental protection, for example); others produce liberal results. For that reason we can assess whether the justices' choices to invalidate or uphold these bureaucratic actions are driven by the underlying policy issue at stake in the litigation.

A. The Standard: Invalidating Administrative Action

1. Majoritarianism, Political Control, and Administrative Agencies

Alexander Hamilton wrote in the Federalist 78 that judges' exercise of "will instead of judgment" would result in the "substitution of their pleasure for that of the legislative body" (Hamilton 1788, 440). This preoccupation with judicial invalidation of legislation has become the focus of most studies and criticisms of judicial activism. As discussed in the preceding chapters, claims of activism most often arise in connection with fears that judicial policy making supplants the judgment of the people's representatives. Far less frequently do observers complain that judicial review of administrative action is activist because it allows judges to impose their own policy preferences on officials acting within administrative agencies.

Perhaps it is not surprising that one hears less often about activism in the administrative/executive context. Bureaucrats are appointed rather than elected, and thus the link between majoritarian preferences and bureaucratic action is far less clear. Invalidating bureaucratic action is therefore less likely to implicate the Court in charges that it is acting in a counter-majoritarian fashion. In contrast, one might argue that judicial review of bureaucratic action itself promotes administrative accountability because judges "guard the guardians" to ensure that these unelected agents do not unlawfully trammel individual due process or other constitutional rights, act outside the scope of their statutory authority, or violate separation of powers principles. In this way, the judiciary actually promotes democratic accountability by ensuring that agencies act in accordance with statutory and constitutional requirements.

While perhaps valid from a theoretical standpoint, this perspective ignores several political realities. First, judges themselves are not elected and thus are not necessarily in the best position to promote accountability and majoritarianism in the executive branch. In fact, at the federal level, many have complained that excessive scrutiny by judges who impose onerous procedural obligations on agencies or who interfere with an agency's interpretation of its governing legislation actually *undermines* democratic accountability by limiting presidential control over administrative outputs. "Th[is] enfeebling of the presidency is in turn blamed for policy stagnation, bureaucratic drift, and erosion of accountability" (Clayton 1994, 845).

Second, administrative agencies are subject to substantial oversight and control by the legislative branch, which created the agencies in the first place to implement the legislative agenda. At the federal level, Congress has several tools at its disposal to shape agency behavior by rewarding actions that conform to congressional preferences and sanctioning those that do not (Balla and Wright 2001). Primary among these tools is Congress's power over the budget: it appropriates funds for agency operations and can tighten the purse strings when the agency fails to fulfill its statutory mandate. In addition, legislative committees oversee agency operations and hold hearings to monitor and investigate agency activities. And members of these committees need not exercise constant vigilance in reviewing administrative agencies' operations; they may rely on interest groups, program clients, and lobbyists to alert them to suboptimal agency performance (McCubbins and Schwartz 1984). Congress may also constrain agencies *ex ante* by imposing procedural obligations that increase the probability that agencies will accommodate the preferences of favored constituencies when formulating administrative policies (McCubbins, Noll, and Weingast 1987). And of course, where the president has the power to appoint agency heads, he may do so only with the Senate's advice and consent.

Social scientific studies have demonstrated convincingly that in many circumstances, congressional control of administrative agencies is quite effective. Using data from the Federal Trade Commission, Weingast and Moran (1983) found that the Commission's decisions varied with the ideological preferences of members of the relevant oversight committees in Congress. Moe's study of the National Labor Relations Board drew similar conclusions (Moe 1985). In their comprehensive study of seven federal agencies, Wood and Waterman (1991) also determined that congressional instruments of control, including revising budgets and oversight, were effective in enabling Congress to manipulate agency decisions and outputs. And in a study of congressional control over the federal bureaucracy by the conservative 104th Congress, Hedge and Johnson (2002) investigated whether the 1994 shift in party dominance from Democratic to Republican was reflected in regulatory policy. The authors' findings were stark: using budgetary and other procedural control mechanisms, the new Republican Congress was able to cause "an immediate decline in regulatory vigor" lasting one or two years. "What is so intriguing," the authors note, "is not that the four agencies responded to congressional pressures (there is no shortage of evidence suggesting that agencies respond to signals from Congress) but that they did so quickly and in the absence of any statutory reason" (Hedge and Johnson 2002, 347).

These studies support the conclusion that administrative agencies do respond to their principals in Congress and thus are not institutions wholly insulated from and unaccountable to the electorate. To be sure, agency accountability to the electorate is somewhat attenuated when it is accomplished through the legislative body. But accountability nonetheless exists. If the legislature represents the majority will and is able to control agency policy making, then agencies themselves arguably constitute "majoritarian" institutions.

Administrative agency action may reflect the popular will not only because agencies may be held politically accountable via the legislature; agencies may also act in furtherance of majority preferences when they respond to and implement the chief executive's policy agenda. In most instances, bureaucrats must respond to two main principals—the legislature and the executive. In that sense, administrative agencies are "doubly" accountable to the people through two institutional pathways.[70]

In the federal government, the president has several powerful mechanisms at his disposal to ensure that federal agencies pursue the administration's policy agenda. Chief among these mechanisms are the appointment and removal of agency heads. Other means also exist for the president to control agencies, however, including regulatory review through the Office of Management and Budget, selection of career executives below the agency head, influence over the budgetary process, and agency reorganization by executive order (Wood and Waterman 1991). Moreover, the empirical evidence indicates that the practical effect of these controls is quite pronounced: even in the case of independent regulatory commissions, Wood and Waterman (1991) found that presidential administrations were successful in shaping regulatory policy outcomes to conform to the president's preferred policies. Other studies have made similar findings (Durant 1992;

---

70. The same can be said for legislative enactments, since the president or governor usually must sign a bill into law. But this is not always so, as occasionally the legislature overrides an executive veto to enact law without his or her consent.

Ringquist 1995). And a survey of executive-level officials in 12 federal executive branch agencies and independent regulatory commissions revealed that agency officials perceived Congress as the most influential principal, with the president close behind (Furlong 1998).

These studies strongly suggest that administrative agencies are not unaccountable, freewheeling institutions, but rather are significantly constrained by their elected principals and thus are at least indirectly accountable to majoritarian preferences. Certainly, at least at the federal level where all judges are appointed for life on good behavior with salaries that cannot be reduced, officials within administrative agencies are far more closely connected to the polity than are the judges reviewing their actions. For that reason, critics of judicial intervention into the administrative process complain that judges' "compulsions" toward onerous procedural requirements and their second-guessing of agency policy choices are antidemocratic and produce a dysfunctional and "fettered presidency" (Rabkin 1989; Crovitz and Rabkin 1989). As Cornell Clayton describes the critics' position regarding judicial scrutiny of agency action: "courts have fettered the administrative process by judicializing rulemaking, by demanding synoptic decision making of administrative agencies, and by refusing to accept agency interpretations of statutory duty" (Clayton 1994, 844). Often these complaints emerge from conservative quarters, where critics claim that a liberal judiciary "used statutory review as a pretext for thwarting the policy agenda of conservative presidents and for imposing their own liberal policy preferences on the bureaucracy" (Clayton 1994, 844).

For these reasons, conservative critics in particular favor deferential judicial review of agency action. Judicial deference to agency decision making is consistent with theories promoting executive branch autonomy, including unitary executive theory. Unitary executive theorists "support a broad presidential power over removal [of agency heads] and control over law execution" (Calabresi and Yoo 1997, 1453). As one of the most prominent supporters of the unitary executive, Justice Scalia has "urged the Supreme Court to adopt new standards of statutory review that would restrict lower court discretion to examine congressional intent and would require maximum deference to executive branch decision making" (Clayton 1994, 844). These complaints about activist review of administrative action thus stem from a theory of clearly delineated powers that maximizes executive branch autonomy to implement laws in accordance with presidential preferences.

Accusations of intrusive judicial review of agency action may be overblown, however, at least as directed at the U.S. Supreme Court. Studies demonstrate that the Court supports agencies at a very high rate, usually about 70% of the time (Canon and Giles 1972; Handberg 1976; Crowley 1987). In part, this level of success could be due to the Solicitor General's influence over whether an agency may petition the Supreme Court to review an adverse ruling; this process screens out those appeals where the government's legal arguments are less convincing. In addition, some have pointed to the deferential standards established in the Administrative Procedure Act (APA)[71] to explain agency success before the federal courts. The APA's standard for judicial review requires reversal of agency action only if it is "arbitrary and capricious" or unsupported by "substantial evidence" (Humphries and Songer 1999, 209).

Researchers have also found, however, that the Court's high level of deference often masks significant ideological differences in the manner in which individual justices approach review of administrative agencies. As Crowley noted, "It is fairly easy to practice judicial restraint and defer to decisions made by an administrative agency if one agrees with the results that the agency has reached. Nevertheless, restraint as a judicial norm takes on real meaning only when a justice defers to another institution despite disagreeing with the policy outcome" (Crowley 1986, 275). When analyzed in the light of the substantive policy outcomes under review, Crowley and others have found that the ideological direction of the policy under review shaped the justices' decisions whether to defer. Liberal justices deferred to the agency when reviewing liberal policy choices, but tended to strike actions that resulted in a conservative outcome, and vice versa for the conservative justices (Sheehan 1992; J. L. Smith 2007; Deen, Ignani, and Meernik 2005).

This standard of activism in review of executive decisions was recently adopted by Thomas Miles and Cass Sunstein (2007). Miles and Sunstein examined the Supreme Court justices' voting patterns from 1989 through 2005 (covering much of the Rehnquist Court) in cases where the Court assessed the legality of decisions by federal agencies. The authors categorized the justices in terms of the frequency with which they invalidated agency action, as well as in terms of their propensity to vote to support action with which they agreed ideologically and strike action with which they disagreed on substantive policy grounds. They found that the most activist justice, in terms of invalidating agency action most frequently, was Justice Scalia, while the most restraintist justice was Justice Breyer. As for ideological influence, the study concluded that the justice who demonstrated the

---

71. 5 U.S.C. §§ 500-706 (West. 2008).

strongest ideological voting pattern was Justice Thomas, while the most ideologically neutral was Justice Kennedy.

The Miles-Sunstein approach has been criticized on a number of grounds that are relevant to the study we undertake here. First, Edward Whelan argued the Miles-Sunstein study was flawed because it presented an inappropriate measure of judicial activism:

> [U]nlike a Supreme Court ruling that finds a federal or state law unconstitutional, a ruling that invalidates federal agency action as contrary to statute does not end the political processes. On the contrary, Congress is free to revise statutory law to permit or even require the same agency action. Further, in the frequent instances in which the agency has merely failed to follow proper procedures, the agency itself is free to redo its work and achieve the same result (Whelan 2007).

Whelan is correct that Court decisions invalidating executive action on grounds that it contradicts a federal statute may be more readily reversed by the legislature or even the executive branch. For example, the Court may find that the executive adoption of a policy failed to follow the procedures required under the APA. In such a case, the agency might yet adopt precisely the same policy by returning to the issue, following the correct legal procedures, and reaching the same outcome. The agency "could return to the court with the same substantive result and the court would have to uphold it" (Garland 1985, 533). In addition, when the Court invalidates an executive action as contrary to substantive statutory authority or direction, Congress may amend the statute to make the action lawful. These majoritarian actions to validate the policy rejected by the Court are unavailable in the case of constitutional rulings, which may technically be reversed only through the very onerous and seldom undertaken approach of adopting a constitutional amendment.

Yet the ease with which Congress can override judicial decisions invalidating agency action is often overstated. Even when Congress disagrees with the Court's invalidation of agency action as inconsistent with statutory limitations (as opposed to constitutional review) it may be too preoccupied with other pressing national issues to override that decision legislatively. A congressional refusal to override judicial action thus does not imply agreement with its result; legislative inaction may simply mean that the Congress had more pressing national priorities to consider.

As Jeffrey Segal has pointed out, considerable transaction and opportunity costs are associated with passing legislation to overturn judicial decisions (Segal 1997, 31). Once Congress unleashes judicial power to moni-tor executive action, it is difficult for the legislature to control the effects of that power. Certain "institutional features of Congress such as its bicameral structure, the committee system, and even the subcommittee system, make it difficult for Congress to overturn a Supreme Court decision" (Maltzman, Spriggs, and Wahlbeck 1999, 48–49). Keith Krehbiel has demonstrated the importance of various "pivot points" that require substantial supermajorities for legislative action, which means that "gridlock" is the "essential reality" of government (Krehbiel 1998, 5). And even if the legislature could act, the meaning of its actions would still be subject to the Court's interpretation; an activist Court might well disregard or manipulate the meaning of the new statute. It is therefore "exceedingly difficult for a majority coalition in Congress to succeed in overturning a judicial decision even where there would not be a majority for enacting the legislation reflecting the Court's decision" (Rodriguez 1992, 224). Thus a judicial ruling on executive authority has activist consequences despite the theoretical possibility of legislative override.

Whelan further complains that, by their very nature, administrative agency decisions are often liberal in orientation, and thus Miles and Sunstein's measure of activism is improperly weighted in favor of finding that conserva-tive justices were more activist than their liberal counterparts. But as Miles and Sunstein indicate, agency action is often challenged by public interest groups as well as business interests; this fact indicates that agency decisions are not uniformly liberal (Miles and Sunstein 2007a) As for concerns that their measure of activism does not control for whether the legal judgment in the individual case was "correct," Miles and Sunstein respond that "an ideal measure of judicial activism would identify the situations in which judges pursue their own ideological goals at the expense of the 'correct' legal out-come" (Miles and Sunstein 2007a). Nevertheless, they observe that the ideo-logical skew in certain justices' voting patterns "suggest[s] that certain justices are, according to this imprecise metric, reaching decisions that were likely not correct" (Miles and Sunstein 2007a).

While we agree with Whelan that administrative agency action differs in kind from legislative action, we think Miles and Sunstein have the better argument. Judicial review of administrative action still implicates concerns that the judiciary will improperly encroach on the prerogatives of the execu-tive branch in furtherance of judges' own policy preferences. In that sense, as Miles and Sunstein point out, patterns of ideological decision making "smack of judicial activism" (Miles and Sunstein 2007a).

2. Sources of Supreme Court Authority to Review
Executive Action

Before we turn to the justices' voting behavior in these cases, we pause for a brief review of the Court's authority to review and invalidate administrative action. Challenges to agency action may be brought on constitutional and/ or statutory grounds. Although such decisions are not common, the Court periodically finds constitutional reasons to invalidate an executive action. In addition, the Court may use its statutory authority to invalidate agency action.

While most of the cases involving constitutional challenges to executive action involve law enforcement, there are also a number of cases in which the decisions of administrative agencies are challenged based on allegations that the action violated constitutional rights. For example, an executive action might be challenged on grounds that it violates citizens' rights to free-dom of speech. Thus, in *Rust v. Sullivan*,[72] a challenge was brought to regula-tions promulgated by the Department of Health and Human Services that prohibited doctors who worked in institutions receiving federal funds from counseling patients about the option of abortion. In *Rust*, the Court upheld the regulations against the First Amendment challenge on grounds that the government may implement value judgments through funding decisions without engaging in viewpoint discrimination.

Alternatively, executive action may be vacated on nonconstitutional grounds. The most common basis for such invalidation is the Administrative Procedure Act (APA). This 1946 statute established a series of procedural requirements for different types of administrative actions. The statute also empowered the judiciary to review administrative actions and vacate them when they were found to be contrary to law, "arbitrary and capricious," or unsupported by "substantial evidence."[73] Although review under the APA was initially quite deferential, in the 1960s and 1970s, courts developed a "hard look" standard for administrative regulation that proved much more activist in assessing and rejecting regulatory actions, especially with respect to envi-ronmental decisions. The courts thus became increasingly willing to invali-date federal administrative actions under the authority of the APA or even force additional agency action (L. A. Smith 1985). As a result, "administrative

---

72. 500 U.S. 173 (1991).

73. 5 U.S.C. § 706 (West 2008).

law became more of a wellspring of judicial activism, strengthening the judiciary's institutional power relative to the executive branch" (Powers and Rothman 2002, 29–30).

Courts also review executive action in accordance with other statutory standards besides the APA. A typical case might challenge agency action as not authorized by the statute that established and empowered the agency. Often, this determination involves whether the agency has properly interpreted its governing statute. The current standard for determining whether the agency's interpretation should be upheld was provided in the important case of *Chevron U.S.A., Inc. v. Natural Resources Defense Council*,[74] which created a method for judicial evaluation of agency decisions and imposed a deferential standard for review of the agency's own interpretation of its enabling statute.

ℱ B. The Voting Behavior of the Individual Justices

To assess judicial activism in the area of administrative review, we used the U.S. Supreme Court Judicial Database to compile a dataset of the Court's decisions reviewing actions by federal administrative agencies. First, we identified a potential pool of cases using the "auth_dec" and "admin" variables. We then reviewed each case to code whether the Court struck or upheld the challenged government action, and whether the basis for the decision rested on constitutional or statutory grounds. To classify the substantive policy at issue in each case, we again relied on the Spaeth directionality codes. We also categorized the cases based on whether they emerged from an independent regulatory commission or an executive branch agency. Unlike executive branch agencies, where the president may dismiss an agency head at will, presidents do not enjoy the authority to dismiss the heads of independent commissions such as the Securities and Exchange Commission or the Equal Employment Opportunity Commission. Because independent commissions were created in this fashion to insulate them from presidential control, Supreme Court justices may indeed treat their decisions with greater deference (Sheehan 1992). For that reason, we thought it prudent to identify them for separate analysis.

---

74. 467 U.S. 837 (1984).

We also note that the Court's agenda in this area has experienced substantial change over time. For example, the Warren Court reviewed a significant number of cases on certain types of issues, including conscientious objector status in military draft disputes and dismissals of Communists from the government, which are not found in the later era. Moreover, the first 20 years saw a large number of cases involving review of the National Labor Relations Board, but these have waned considerably over time. To consider changes in the Court's behavior in these cases over time, therefore, we calculated the number of challenges to federal administrative action in each term, and the number of actions that were actually invalidated. These figures are presented in Figure 13.

These time series data demonstrate two trends. First, the Supreme Court has been extremely deferential to federal administrative action over time, with only a small proportion of such actions invalidated in each term. Second, the trend in terms of challenges considered and percent invalidated comprised a fairly similar pattern throughout the Warren and Burger Courts. In the Rehnquist Court, however, the trend changes, with substantially fewer cases heard by the Court and a concomitant decrease in the frequency of invalidations. This latter trend is consistent with the Rehnquist Court's substantially diminished docket.

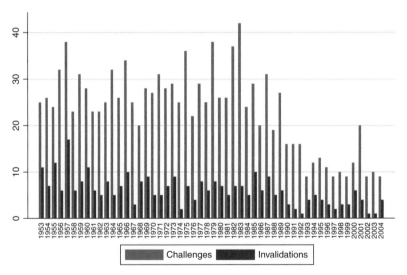

FIGURE 13 Challenges to and Invalidations of Federal Administrative Action, per Court Term

1. The Frequency of the Justices' Votes to Strike Executive Action

We begin with an overall review of the justices' votes to strike federal executive actions in general, regardless of the type of challenge (constitutional or statutory) or the type of agency (independent or executive). The rates at which the justices voted to strike federal action over the course of their individual careers on the Warren, Burger, and Rehnquist Court are set forth in Figure 14, which ranks the justices in terms of their propensity to strike administrative action once a challenge has been brought before the Court.

The graph makes clear that most justices voted to invalidate federal administrative action within a very narrow range of probability: between 26 and 42%. This reflects the overall level of deference that was apparent in Figure 13. Two justices stand out, however. Perhaps not surprisingly, Justice Douglas is the most activist in this area, voting to strike federal action more than half the time, while Justice White is extremely deferential, voting to strike in only one case out of five. Contemporary conservatives like Justices Scalia and Thomas appear quite activist, though Justice Rehnquist was relatively deferential. These findings are generally consistent with those of Miles and Sunstein, who identified Scalia as the most activist justice, but we find that Thomas was even more activist than Scalia. Like Miles and Sunstein, we also find that Breyer is quite restrained, but so are Ginsburg and Souter.

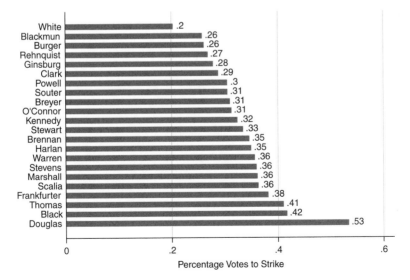

FIGURE 14 Percent Votes to Strike Federal Administrative Action 1953 to 2004 Terms

These differences could result from our inclusion of constitutional and statutory cases in the data presented in Figure 14. We also considered votes in all cases, while Miles and Sunstein limited their evaluation to votes involving deference under the *Chevron* doctrine.

To assess whether differences exist between the justices' propensity to invalidate action challenged on constitutional as opposed to statutory grounds, we separated their votes into the types of legal challenges made to the administrative action. The proportion of votes each justice cast to strike federal action on constitutional and on statutory grounds is presented in Table 8.

Given the deferential standard of review prescribed by the Administrative Procedure Act, one might expect that constitutional challenges would provide the justices with more substantial legal reasons to strike administrative action than statutory challenges. Yet it is not clear from the table that constitutional challenges elicit less deference from the justices. Several liberal justices are less deferential in constitutional cases, including Douglas, Black,

TABLE 8 Percentage of Votes to Strike Federal Administrative Action 1953–2004

Justice	Percentage to Strike Federal Action Constitutional	Number of Votes	Percentage to Strike Federal Action Statutory	Number of Votes
Black	58.82	17	41.07	448
Blackmun	25.00	80	25.90	502
Brennan	49.44	89	32.96	804
Breyer	37.50	8	30.48	105
Burger	18.84	69	27.39	398
Clark	11.11	9	29.23	366
Douglas	80.00	30	51.80	529
Frankfurter	20.00	5	38.60	228
Ginsburg	11.11	9	29.20	113
Harlan	23.53	17	35.43	398
Kennedy	25.00	16	33.00	203
Marshall	55.00	80	33.20	506
O'Connor	29.55	44	31.51	365
Powell	19.67	61	32.52	326
Rehnquist	13.25	83	28.79	580
Scalia	36.36	22	36.29	237
Souter	45.45	11	29.49	156
Stevens	31.25	64	36.57	495
Stewart	33.93	56	33.40	512
Thomas	40.00	10	41.13	141
Warren	36.36	11	35.61	410
White	17.44	86	20.69	691

Marshall, Brennan, Souter, and Breyer. But it appears that conservative justices are *more* deferential in constitutional cases than in statutory ones, or vote about the same way in each type of case. Thus Rehnquist is more likely to vote to strike when a statutory challenge is brought, as are Kennedy and Powell. O'Connor, Thomas, Scalia, and Stewart vote to strike at about the same rate in both types of cases. This result could stem from liberals' greater sensitivity and willingness to protect civil liberties in the face of adverse government action. Moreover, these results should be interpreted with some caution, given the small number of constitutional votes available for analysis for several of the justices in Table 8.

2. Distinguishing Between Independent Regulatory Commissions and Executive Branch Agencies

We see a similar difference between the voting behavior of liberals and conservatives when we separate their votes into two alternative groups: votes in cases challenging action by independent regulatory commissions and votes in cases challenging action by executive branch agencies. The probabilities that the justices would vote to strike action by the two agency types are presented in Table 9. Liberal justices show some tendency to defer more often to the actions of independent regulatory commissions than to executive branch agencies. Thus Marshall, Brennan, Stevens, Douglas, Ginsburg, and Souter all voted to strike the actions of independent agencies at a lower rate. In contrast, Powell, Rehnquist, Scalia, and Thomas were more deferential to the executive branch than to the independent commissions. This finding is consistent with prior research (Lindquist, Smith, and Cross 2007), and may reflect the conservatives' preference for presidential control and a unitary executive. The independence of regulatory commissions is at odds with the notion that all executive power should be consolidated squarely in the executive branch under the control and domination of the president. For that reason, conservatives may be predisposed to skepticism regarding the actions of independent agencies.

3. The Voting Behavior of Individual Justices as Influenced by Ideology

While these frequencies and proportions are revealing, result-oriented judging is the most telling measure of judicial activism as we have

TABLE 9 Percentage of Votes to Strike Federal Action, Controlling for Agency Type 1953–2004

Justice	Percentage to Strike Action by Independent Agencies (N)	Number of Votes	Percentage to Strike Action by Executive Agencies (N)	Number of Votes
Black	39.92	253	42.50	200
Blackmun	25.00	228	25.37	339
Brennan	30.00	420	38.38	456
Breyer	27.91	43	31.34	67
Burger	28.50	193	24.06	266
Clark	30.23	215	25.32	154
Douglas	45.82	299	61.44	246
Frankfurter	37.90	124	37.25	102
Ginsburg	23.40	47	29.17	72
Harlan	35.00	220	33.33	174
Kennedy	29.33	75	33.33	138
Marshall	30.34	234	39.16	332
O'Connor	31.08	148	31.50	254
Powell	34.23	149	27.04	233
Rehnquist	30.59	255	24.24	396
Scalia	39.33	89	34.15	164
Souter	23.73	59	33.65	104
Stevens	30.19	212	38.87	337
Stewart	35.09	285	31.14	273
Thomas	45.28	53	37.89	95
Warren	35.00	240	35.67	171
White	21.93	342	18.18	420

conceptualized it. Therefore to assess whether the justices' votes were shaped by their personal preferences regarding the substantive policy content embodied in these agency decisions, we calculated the percentage of votes each cast to strike and uphold liberal agency action. These figures are provided in Table 10.

The results show ideological differences roughly similar to those found in the earlier chapters. Justices who showed a relatively strong propensity to cast votes that promoted liberal policy outcomes were Marshall, Brennan, Warren, Douglas, Black, and Clark. For these justices, ideological skewing was fairly pronounced, with ideology usually manifesting itself most strongly in votes to strike rather than to uphold. The same pattern of ideological votes to strike is also evident in the case of some of the conservative justices. Thus Justices Rehnquist, Burger, Powell and Thomas were more likely to cast conservative votes to strike liberal policies than they were to cast votes to uphold

TABLE 10 Ideological Direction of Votes to Strike Federal Administrative Action 1953–2004

Justice	Percentage to Strike Federal Action	Votes to Strike: Percent Liberal	Votes to Uphold: Percent Liberal	Number of Votes*
Black	41.72	78.65	71.22	463
Blackmun	25.77	60.00	47.79	574
Brennan	34.60	74.43	60.31	887
Breyer	30.90	54.29	54.43	114
Burger	26.12	34.71	40.58	466
Clark	28.80	63.89	58.05	375
Douglas	53.30	69.02	72.80	558
Frankfurter	38.19	59.09	50.00	232
Ginsburg	27.86	52.94	52.81	123
Harlan	34.93	46.36	48.67	401
Kennedy	32.42	45.07	43.15	217
Marshall	36.17	78.33	59.84	574
O'Connor	31.29	44.09	37.77	405
Powell	30.49	30.51	38.66	387
Rehnquist	26.84	23.73	36.31	659
Scalia	36.29	40.86	37.80	257
Souter	30.53	60.78	50.00	167
Stevens	36.95	58.71	49.58	556
Stewart	33.45	47.37	57.85	568
Thomas	41.05	27.42	36.67	152
Warren	35.62	75.84	67.53	420
White	20.33	53.12	48.86	772

* The figures in this column differ from those in the general table for votes to strike administrative action (Table 8) because a few votes could not be categorized in ideological terms.

a liberal policy. Other conservatives, including Scalia and O'Connor, demonstrated relatively conservative voting behavior (they were much less likely to vote to uphold liberal policies), but they were nonetheless more neutral than Rehnquist and Thomas.

Other justices did not demonstrate much of an ideological bent to their voting behavior, casting about equal percentages of liberal votes to strike and uphold administrative action. The liberals of the contemporary Court era, for example, are not ideologically activist in this area. Justices such as Ginsburg, Souter, and Breyer show little in the way of liberal skewing in their votes in these administrative cases. Among more conservative justices, Kennedy is also fairly neutral in his voting behavior. Other neutral justices include White, Blackmun, Stevens, Stewart, Harlan, and Frankfurter.

As in the preceding chapters, based on the statistics presented in the preceding tables and graphs, we categorize the justices in terms of their levels of **institutional activism** and **ideological activism**, as set forth in Table 11. As before, we rank justices high on the institutional activism dimension when they are less willing to defer to other governmental actors; this dimension is based on the simple proportion of the justices' votes to strike administrative action overall. We rank justices high on the ideological activism dimension when they demonstrate a pronounced tendency to vote ideologically in these cases. Justices in the upper left quadrant strike administrative action at a fairly high rate and vote ideologically in administrative cases. Justices in the upper right quadrant are less deferential to the executive branch but are not ideologically motivated. Justices in the lower left quadrant are ideologically motivated but deferential. Justices in the lower right quadrant are the "restraintists" in this area; they are not particularly ideological in their voting behavior and they defer to the executive branch.

Among the justices in the restraintist quadrant are the Clinton appointees Ginsburg and Breyer, as well as Justices Souter and Kennedy. Breyer and Kennedy were also identified by Miles and Sunstein for their restraintist (in the case of Breyer) and nonideological (in the case of Kennedy) voting behavior.

TABLE 11 Taxonomy of Judicial Behavior—Votes to Invalidate Federal Executive Action

Institutional Activism	Ideological Activism	
	High	Low
High	Marshall	Stevens
	Brennan	Harlan
	Thomas	Frankfurter
	Scalia	
	Warren	
	Douglas	
	Black	
Low	Powell	White
	Rehnquist	Blackmun
	Burger	Breyer
	Clark	Souter
	O'Connor	Ginsburg
		Stewart
		Kennedy

✇ C. Conclusion

The invalidation of executive branch actions is too often overlooked as a dimension of judicial activism, with the focus usually going to constitutional invalidation of legislative enactments. Yet the executive branch is also a majoritarian institution to the extent it responds to the preferences of its principals in Congress and the presidency. And many administrative agencies are staffed with employees who have developed technical expertise in the policy area covered by the agency's jurisdiction. As Bradley Canon points out in his dimensional analysis of activism, when the Court second-guesses agencies, it may constitute activism if "the nature of the policy is such that choices are better informed by data or expertise not normally available in the judicial process" (Canon 1983, 247). For these reasons, judicial review of administrative decisions is a critical element in any multidimensional analysis of judicial activism.

Perhaps because agencies are often staffed with experts who make decisions in areas that fall outside the scope of most judges' knowledge, as well as because of relatively deferential legal standards of review, we find that the Supreme Court has exercised its power of judicial review over administrative action with considerable restraint. With one exception, all the justices whose votes we analyzed chose to strike agency decisions only around 30% of the time.[75] On the other hand, as we found with review of legislative enactments, for many of the justices in our sample, ideology plays an important role in their decisions whether to vote to strike agency action or uphold it. In this sense, we were able to identify justices whose decisions appeared more activist than their more ideologically neutral colleagues on the Court.

---

75. Some have argued that the Court has demonstrated a distinctive deference to the president over the course of its history, largely because "a Court not in step with the President's political agenda was vulnerable to political attack" (Silverstein and Ginsberg 1987, 375).

SIX

Justiciability and Judicial Activism

THUS FAR WE HAVE evaluated activism on the U.S. Supreme Court in connection with the Court's power to review the legality of legislative and executive action, focusing our attention on the implications of that power for majoritarianism and the separation of powers. As discussed in Chapter 2, judicial activism is a multidimensional concept that includes a number of elements that may be measured empirically. In addition to invalidating decisions by other governmental actors, which is perhaps the "canonical" definition of judicial activism, judges may also render decisions that enhance the power of the judiciary itself by simply expanding judges' authority to hear disputes. Although certain judge-created "justiciability" standards place limitations on who may bring claims in federal courts, the Court always has the power to liberalize those standards to allow access to favored interests. When the Court lowers justiciability thresholds to the federal courts, it admits parties and interests that look to the courts as "important institutional allies" (Silverstein and Ginsberg 1987, 387). A Court interested in stamping its imprint on public policy would "open the door, thus allowing it a greater volume of cases with which to shape . . . doctrine" (Taggart and DeZee 1985, 92). Easing the standards by which litigants may bring their claims in federal court therefore "enhance[s] the potential for an expanded judicial role in the policy-making process" (Silverstein and Ginsberg 1987, 379). For that reason, in Chapter 2 we discussed this dimension of judicial activism under the heading "institutional aggrandizement."

Institutional aggrandizement through the Court's gatekeeping function can take another form as well. The Court can also increase its impact on policy outcomes by expanding its discretionary docket. Quite simply, the more cases the Court takes, the more it can determine litigants' rights and responsibilities, and the more opportunity it has to shape existing doctrinal standards or to generate new ones. Since 1925, the Court has exercised almost complete discretion over its own docket via the writ of certiorari.[76] One might argue, then, that an expansive docket—simply in terms of the number of cases decided—reflects a more activist Court. Henry Hart's criticism of Warren Court activism, for example, produced his recommendation that the justices exercise restraint by simply deciding fewer cases each term (Hart 1959, 100–101).

In this chapter, we begin with a brief description of the Court's docket from the Warren to the Rehnquist Courts. Although the size of the Court's docket can reveal some information about the justices' willingness to expand the Court's influence or power, we believe the more telling measure involves the justices' votes to grant or deny access pursuant to justiciability standards. As Taggart and DeZee noted years ago, decisions to grant the writ of certiorari "are rather narrow in controlling access when considered in light of the Court's second gatekeeping power [to grant or deny access under doctrines of justiciability]" (Taggart and DeZee 1985, 84). For that reason, we focus our analysis on those doctrinal votes, evaluating the frequency with which the justices voted to grant access pursuant to the various justiciability rules, as well as the extent to which those votes have been shaped by the justices' policy preferences.

❦ A. The Standard: Granting Access to the Federal Courts

1. The Supreme Court's Caseload over Time

We begin with a brief examination of the Court's caseload over time, reflecting as it does the justices' power over the Court's discretionary docket. Figure 15 presents the number of signed opinions issued by year, and demonstrates clearly that the size of the Supreme Court's docket varied substantially from 1953 to 2004. The data indicate a strong upward trend in the 1970s, followed by a precipitous drop during the Rehnquist Court. Scholars are divided over

---

76. Prior to 1925, the Court was required to hear a large number of cases by right of appeal. In 1925, however, Congress passed a Judiciary Act that substantially reduced the right to appeal to the U.S. Supreme Court and thus reduced the Court's mandatory docket. Judiciary Act of 1925, 43 Stat. 936 (1925). In 1988, Congress eliminated most of the remaining mandatory appeals. Review of Cases by the Supreme Court, Pub. L. No. 100-352, 102 Stat. 662 (1988). Even prior to 1988, however, the Court was able to circumvent its mandatory caseload de facto by deciding mandatory appeals summarily and without oral argument (Cordray and Cordray 2001; Hellman 1985).

explanations for these noticeable shifts. One explanation for the increase in the 1970s is that the Court changed its oral argument procedures in 1970 to reduce the parties' argument time from one hour to a half-hour for each side, thus making additional time available to hear more cases (Cordray and Cordray 2001, 740). The Court also reorganized its argument schedule to take up fewer days each week. According to the Cordrays, these changes produced a substantial increase in the Court's reviewing capacity that "presumably encouraged the Court to expand its plenary docket over the course of Chief Justice Burger's tenure" (Cordray and Cordray 2001, 740–741).

Following Burger's retirement, the Court's docket declined dramatically under the leadership of Chief Justice Rehnquist. This change could be due in part to the change in Rehnquist's own behavior. Upon his elevation to chief justice, Rehnquist became less likely to vote to grant certiorari, perhaps because he shifted his focus to institutional rather than personal ideological concerns (Cross and Lindquist 2006). Other justices may have followed his leadership by voting to grant certiorari less often as well. Other explanations focus on the Court's changing personnel, in particular pointing to the 1993 retirement of Justice White. White believed that the Supreme Court failed to resolve circuit court conflicts frequently enough to ensure uniformity in federal law, and thus he voted to grant the writ of certiorari in many cases where it was denied by the other justices (Scott 2006). Indeed, in his recent statistical analysis of the Court's docket, Scott (2006) concluded that the retirements

FIGURE 15 Cases Decided with Signed Opinions by Supreme Court, 1953 to 2004

of Justices White and Blackmun were the most likely cause of the Rehnquist Court's diminishing docket, since both voted to grant certiorari far more often than their colleagues.

We do not undertake an analysis of the justices' votes to grant certiorari here; the data limitations on such an endeavor currently are substantial for the time period we analyze. But variation in the Court's caseload over time, and the findings of existing research, suggest that the Court's docket is indeed shaped by individual justices' perspectives on the Court's proper role in policing the lower federal courts and in resolving policy disputes. Most observers believe that internal forces unique to the sitting justices have influenced the size of the Court's docket, as opposed to forces external to the Court, such as the litigation environment or changes in statutory law governing rights to appeal (Hellman 1996; Cordray and Cordray 2001; O'Brien 2005). In this regard, Tom Merrill identifies Justice Scalia as the potential change agent that may explain the Rehnquist Court's shrinking plenary docket. After arguing that Justice Rehnquist himself was not particularly known to prefer a reduced docket (and had even called for more cases to be decided in earlier terms), Merrill asserts that

> [i]n contrast, we know from published reports that Justice Scalia, from his early years on the Court, strongly favored reducing the number of cases heard by the Court in order to allow more time for each case and improve the quality of the Court's deliberations. We also know, based on docket sheets released as part of Justice Marshall's papers, that Justice Scalia voted to grant review less frequently than any other Justice on the first Rehnquist Court through the 1990 Term. Although Scalia joined the Court at the same time as Rehnquist was elevated to the Chief Justiceship, Scalia's voice on certiorari policy was a new one. Thus, it is my opinion, although I admit it is only an educated guess, that Justice Scalia is the change agent here. In other words, when Justice Scalia joined the Court in 1986, he threw himself with typical gusto into the effort to convince the Justices to adopt a more restrictive standard of review (Merrill 2003, 643–644).

Merrill's observation reflects the idea that individual justices may not only have different attitudes about whether to grant certiorari in individual cases, but also about whether the Court should be granting fewer appeals and thus restricting the impact of the Court as an institution. Justice Scalia, in particular, may prefer a more constrained approach to judicial power.

2. Doctrines of Justiciability

The attitudes of individual justices about allowing access to the Court through discretionary decisions to grant certiorari may accord with their perspectives on whether litigants have met the *legal standards* required to have their cases resolved in federal court. The latter gatekeeping power involves doctrines of court access that determine the circumstances under which plaintiffs' claims may be heard by the judicial branch. Justices' votes to grant or deny access pursuant to these threshold doctrines may turn on their view of the judiciary's proper role and institutional capacity. Lenient application of justiciability standards expands the Court's power to resolve disputes and thus may be considered more activist.

Justiciability doctrines primarily stem from language in Article III of the Constitution, which limits federal court jurisdiction to certain types of "cases" or "controversies." From these two words, the Court has developed a number of justiciability (or "threshold") doctrines that delineate the types of parties who may bring claims in federal court. The core justiciability requirements for federal court review are that plaintiffs demonstrate a live dispute, a personal injury, and the availability of a judicial remedy.

Whether a case is "justiciable" often involves considerations of standing, mootness, and ripeness. To establish "standing," a party must show that it has suffered an "injury in fact," that this injury is fairly traceable to the defendant's actions, and that the injury may be redressed by judicial decree.[77] The Court's 1992 decision in *Lujan v. Defenders of Wildlife*[78] provides a useful example. In *Lujan*, environmental organizations filed suit against the federal government, arguing that regulations promulgated by the Department of the Interior should have ensured that federal funding of activities in foreign countries did not harm endangered species under the Endangered Species Act of 1973.[79] The government moved for summary judgment on grounds that the plaintiffs had not demonstrated sufficient injury to establish standing because they had no concrete interest or connection to the species identified in the suit. The Court agreed, holding that since members of the plaintiff organizations could not demonstrate that they had any concrete injury stemming from the government's action, they could not bring suit in

---

77. *Lujan v. Defenders of Wildlife*, 504 U.S. 555, 560–561 (1992).

78. *Id.*

79. Endangered Species Act of 1973, 16 U.S.C. §§ 1531-1544 (West 2008).

federal court. In particular, the plaintiffs had not sufficiently alleged that they had visited the affected countries and were actively involved in observing or otherwise interacting with the endangered species. Their "generalized" grievance regarding global and local ecosystem destruction was insufficient to provide the specific personal injury necessary to establish standing.

A related doctrine governs claims that have become moot. Occasionally, events occur during the course of litigation that change the plaintiff's circumstances and make it impossible for the Court to provide effective relief on the initial claim. Thus, in *DeFunis v. Odegaard*,[80] the plaintiff sued the University of Washington on grounds that he had been unconstitutionally denied admission to the university's law school on the basis of his race (he was a white applicant complaining of the law school's affirmative action admissions policies). The state trial court agreed with the plaintiff and ordered his admission to law school, and he began his studies there. Although the Washington Supreme Court reversed the trial court's judgment, the university agreed to allow DeFunis to continue his education while the U.S. Supreme Court considered his appeal. By the time the Supreme Court was ready to hear the appeal, DeFunis was in his final semester. Since his alleged injury had already been effectively relieved by his admission to the University of Washington and nearly completed course of studies there, a judgment on his behalf by the Supreme Court could no longer redress his grievance. Consequently, the Court dismissed the case as moot.

There are several important exceptions to the mootness doctrine. First, had DeFunis brought his claim as a class action, dismissal may have been avoided if other members of the class faced similar adverse admissions decisions. Second, the Court has created an important exception to the mootness doctrine for circumstances that are "capable of repetition, yet evading review."[81] When a pregnant woman challenges an abortion restriction, for example, it is inevitable that the litigation will last longer than the pregnancy. The child's birth technically renders any such challenge moot, since a judicial order allowing the abortion would then have no effect on the particular plaintiff's circumstances. Yet pregnancies may occur more than once, and thus are capable of repetition. The relatively short gestation period, however, creates a situation where regulations affecting abortion rights would "evade review" if mootness doctrines were strictly applied. For these practical

---

80. 416 U.S. 312 (1974).

81. *Southern Pacific Terminal Co. v. Interstate Commerce Commission*, 219 U.S. 498, 514 (1911).

reasons, the Court allows such cases to go forward even when they are technically moot.[82]

This exception provides the Court with considerable discretion in determining whether a case has been rendered moot by changing circumstances. For example, the Court resolved a recent challenge to a school district's assignment of children to public schools based on their race, even though the school district in question had ceased the use of its race-based student assignment plan, arguably rendering the dispute moot.[83] The majority reasoned that, absent a contrary ruling, the district could resume its plan at any time and thus the challenged action was capable of repetition. The Court thus agreed to review the challenge and struck down the assignment plan on Equal Protection grounds.

The principle of ripeness also limits access to the federal courts. Ripeness constitutes the "flip side" of mootness, in the sense that it precludes review of cases where the plaintiff has not yet experienced a sufficiently concrete injury caused by the defendant's actions. In *Laird v. Tatum*,[84] for example, the plaintiffs complained that a domestic surveillance system developed by the Army in connection with civil disorders during the 1960s chilled their constitutional rights to free speech. But the plaintiffs could not demonstrate that they had yet been surveilled or point to any specific clandestine activities that affected them directly. As a result, the Court found that the case was not yet ripe for judicial review.

The goal of the ripeness doctrine is not necessarily to preclude federal judicial review altogether; rather, it is often used to postpone review until the factual record is better developed. For example, the Court has found that the denial of permission to develop land cannot be evaluated as an unconstitutional taking of private property until all regulatory processes have been completed, allowing the regulatory agencies to make a final decision on the proposed development.[85] And as with other justiciability doctrines, there are exceptions to the ripeness doctrine that provide the justices with considerable discretion in its application. For example, the Court may resolve an

---

82. E.g. *Davis v. Federal Election Commission*, 128 S.Ct. 2759 (2008) (finding challenge to campaign finance reform law "capable of repetition yet evading review"); *Federal Election Com'n v. Wisconsin Right To* Life, Inc., 127 S.Ct. 2652 (2007) (same).

83. *Parents Involved in Community Schools v. Seattle School Dis. No. 1*, 551 U.S. __, 127 S.Ct. 2738 (2007).

84. 408 U.S. 1 (1972).

85. *Palazzolo v. Rhode Island*, 533 U.S. 606 (2001).

unripe dispute if delay would cause undue hardship to one of the parties. If the issues in the case are primarily legal such that greater factual development would not assist their resolution, the Court may also choose to decide the case even if the facts are not fully known.

In addition to standing, mootness, and ripeness, the Court has developed another justiciability doctrine that is not related to constitutional case or controversy requirements, but which nevertheless allows the Court to avoid certain issues when resolution is more properly achieved in the elected branches. The "political question doctrine" is sometimes considered "prudential" rather than constitutional because it reflects the Court's judgment that judicial review would be "imprudent" when it would infringe on the authority of other governmental actors or when courts lack the institutional capacity to resolve the issue most effectively. Examples include the Court's decision not to interfere in impeachment proceedings in Congress or with foreign relations decisions rendered by the president.

In total, these justiciability doctrines provide the Court with the legal means to avoid resolving many disputes. However, these doctrines do not present bright-line rules. Moreover, sufficient exceptions to the doctrinal standards exist to enable the Court to expand or contract their application depending on the circumstances. As Justice Frankfurter observed, justiciability is "not a legal concept with a fixed content or susceptible of scientific verification" but instead is determined by "many subtle pressures, including the appropriateness of the issues for decision by this Court and the actual hardship to the litigants of denying them the relief sought."[86] Indeed, perhaps because of their malleability, the Warren, Burger, and Rehnquist Courts have applied justiciability standards differently over time, thus easing or enhancing their impact depending on the sitting justices' preferences regarding the Court's institutional authority and power, as well as their preferences regarding the underlying substantive claims in the suit. We now turn to a brief history of these trends since 1953.

3. The Court's Approach to Justiciability from the Warren to the Rehnquist Court

During the Warren Court, the justices substantially loosened justiciability standards. According to Silverstein and Ginsberg, "The Warren Court of the

---

86. *Poe v. Ullman*, 367 U.S. 497, 508–509 (1961).

1960s systematically dismantled the complex web of rules and constraints that had limited the scope of judicial power" (Silverstein and Ginsberg 1987, 377). These authors concluded that the Warren Court lowered threshold requirements to further the interests of certain political forces favoring progressive causes including racial equality, environmental protection, and criminal rights. "The justices of the Warren Court were not unaware of the basic fact that liberalization of the case and controversy requirement gave a wider range of litigants access to the courts, and thus rendered a wider range of issues subject to judicial determination" (Silverstein and Ginsberg 1987, 379).

Prominent examples of the Warren Court's rulings to expand access to the federal courts include *Flast v. Cohen*,[87] in which the Court liberalized the rules regarding taxpayer standing to allow challenges to federal expenditures that allegedly violated the First Amendment's Establishment Clause. In *Baker v. Carr*,[88] discussed in Chapter 2, the Court reversed a 1946 precedent that barred plaintiffs from bringing federal court challenges to state legislative apportionment under the political question doctrine. Similarly, in *Powell v. McCormack*,[89] the Court held that the political question doctrine did not preclude Congressman Adam Clayton Powell, Jr. from challenging his exclusion from the House of Representatives. The Warren Court's relaxation of justiciability requirements was often undertaken in the interests of parties seeking to achieve progressive social and political change.

Although many expected retrenchment by the Burger Court with respect to access to the federal courts, comparative studies of the Warren and Burger Courts demonstrated "a very similar pattern of opening access to the judiciary" (Taggart and DeZee 1985). For example, the Burger Court granted standing to public interest groups challenging regulatory actions in cases like *United States v. Students Challenging Regulatory Agency Procedures (SCRAP)*.[90] In *SCRAP*, the Court considered a challenge to Interstate Commerce Commission (ICC) rules allowing an increase in nationwide railroad freight rates for recycled materials on grounds that the rate increase would undermine recycling efforts. By diminishing the movement of recycled materials in favor of raw materials, the plaintiffs claimed they were personally injured by the ICC-approved rate increase because it would adversely

---

87. 392 U.S. 83 (1968).

88. 369 U.S. 186 (1962).

89. 395 U.S. 486 (1969).

90. 412 U.S. 669 (1973).

affect the environment. Although the link between the increased rates and the plaintiffs' injuries was attenuated, and although the injury itself was quite small, the Burger Court nevertheless granted the students standing to sue (Pierce, Shapiro, and Verkuil 2004, 148).

Other rulings by the Burger Court, however, were less hospitable to progressive plaintiff groups. Thus, in *Simon v. Eastern Kentucky Welfare Rights Organization*,[91] civil rights groups challenged a decision of the Internal Revenue Service extending favorable tax treatment to hospitals that chose not to serve indigents to the extent of the hospitals' financial ability. According to the plaintiffs, this taxation rule "encouraged" hospitals to deny services to indigents. The Court denied the plaintiffs standing, however, on grounds that invalidating the Service's ruling would not necessarily redress the plaintiffs' alleged injury. In denying standing, the majority concluded that any causal relationship between the favorable tax treatment and denial of treatment to indigents was simply too speculative.

Although one commentator has claimed that justiciability issues have "remained largely dormant in the last decade [from 1996 to 2006]" (A. M. Siegel 2006, 1107 n.39), the Rehnquist Court had issued several restrictive rulings in prior years. For example, in *Lujan v. Defenders of Wildlife*,[92] discussed above, the Court interpreted the standing requirements strictly by mandating a stronger showing of personal injury. And in the Pledge of Allegiance case *Elk Grove Unified School District v. Newdow*,[93] the Court denied standing to a students' father challenging the pledge as a violation of the Establishment Clause; interestingly, several conservative justices, including Rehnquist, voted to grant standing and thus would have reached the merits of the claim and likely upheld the pledge of allegiance against the constitutional challenge. And in *Shaw v. Reno*,[94] the conservative bloc on the Rehnquist Court, over vigorous dissents by the Court's more liberal justices, held that white plaintiffs living in a racially gerrymandered district had standing to challenge the district's boundaries under the Equal Protection Clause. These latter two cases illustrate that even conservative justices are

---

91. 426 U.S. 26 (1976).

92. 504 U.S. 555 (1992).

93. 542 U.S. 1 (2004).

94. 509 U.S. 630 (1993).

willing to grant standing when it allows them to reach their preferred outcome on the merits.

This brief history reveals the varying approaches the Supreme Court has taken over time to the interpretation of justiciability standards. Obviously, different personnel on the Court view access questions differently; some favor greater access, some less, but often the justices' reactions to justiciability issues turn on their preferences regarding the parties bringing suit. Thus the Warren Court granted access to civil rights litigants, the Rehnquist Court to plaintiffs challenging affirmative action.

✄ B. The Justices' Voting Behavior in Justiciability Cases

1. The Frequency of the Justices' Votes to Grant Access

Supreme Court justices' votes to grant or deny access to the federal courts have attracted the attention of a number of scholars who study judicial behavior quantitatively. In a study of the justices' votes on justiciability between 1953 and 1978, for example, Atkins and Taggart (1984) found that the most "pro-access" justices were Douglas, Black, Fortas, Marshall, Warren, and Brennan. Another study examined the first seven years of the Burger Court and again found that liberal justices, and especially Justice Douglas, were more likely to grant access than their conservative brethren (Rathjen and Spaeth 1979).

We undertake a similar analysis of the justices' votes in justiciability cases from 1953 to 2004. To identify these cases, we relied on issue codes in the U.S. Supreme Court Judicial Database reflecting whether the Court addressed legal questions related to the justiciability doctrines discussed above (issue codes 731, 801–811). We then calculated the proportion of pro-access votes for each justice. Those data are presented in Figure 16.

Figure 16 reveals a pattern similar to that found by Atkins and Taggart (1984) and Rathjen and Spaeth (1979). Clearly, liberal justices are more inclined to grant access to the federal courts than are conservative justices. Leading the group in pro-access votes are Justices Douglas, Warren, Black, Brennan, and Marshall. The most restraintist justices by this measure are conservative justices Scalia, Burger, Thomas, Powell, and Rehnquist. Swing voters Kennedy and O'Connor are somewhat more restrained in this regard than are modern Court liberals Breyer, Souter, and Ginsburg.

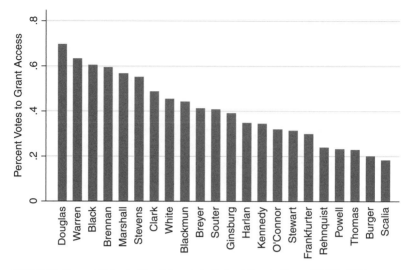

FIGURE 16 Percent Votes to Grant Access to Federal Courts Terms 1953 to 2004

2. The Votes of the Individual Justices as Influenced by Ideology

The data presented in Figure 16 do not, however, account for the ideological dimension of the underlying claims. Indeed, to the extent that justices grant access to groups they favor politically, and deny access to those they disfavor, the simple proportion of votes to grant access may mask an important ideological dimension to the justices' voting behavior. Moreover, decisions to deny access often produce conservative results simply because claimants seeking access in these cases typically seek more progressive legal policies (Rathjen and Spaeth 1979). For that reason, conservative justices' apparent restraint could simply result from their preference for conservative outcomes.

Several existing studies indicate that the justices vote to grant or deny access strategically in order to reach ideologically preferred outcomes. For example, a study of five major Supreme Court standing rulings of the 1990s found that 31 of the 33 justices' votes could be explained ideologically based on the underlying substantive policy issue in the case (Pierce 1999). Another analysis of Supreme Court environmental decisions found that the conservative justices used justiciability as "institutional restraint" in pursuit of pro-development "policy activism" (Levy and Glicksman 1989, 421). Chae (2000) reached similar conclusions in a follow-up study of environmental decisions. Thus it has been suggested that "denials of standing will typically ensure that conservative policies prevail" in some significant cases (Klein 2008, 1236–1237).

On the other hand, granting access may also serve conservative interests when the complaining parties seek judgments invalidating liberal policies. For example, as noted above, in *Shaw v. Reno* the conservative justices on the Rehnquist Court granted standing to plaintiffs challenging affirmative action in legislative redistricting, thus allowing a conservative result on the merits. When the Court manipulates justiciability doctrines to reach desired policy results, those doctrines "can hardly be viewed as a significant limit" on the exercise of judicial power (Wolfe 1997, 80).

To evaluate whether the justices' votes to grant access depend on the types of underlying substantive claims brought by the plaintiffs, we classified each case in terms of the substantive policy content of the underlying lawsuit, using the coding scheme developed by Harold Spaeth in connection with the U.S Supreme Court Judicial Database. Thus when a justice voted to deny access to a progressive group (and to grant access to a conservative litigant), the vote was coded as conservative. We followed the same procedure to classify liberal votes.[95] For each justice, we then calculated the percentage of votes to grant access where the vote to grant would favor liberal claimants, and the percentage of votes to grant access where vote to grant would favor those bringing more conservative claims. As an example, again consider *Shaw*. In that case, the majority granted access to the plaintiffs challenging the state's redistricting plan; these votes were coded as promoting a conservative outcome on the merits because they allowed plaintiffs challenging affirmative action to sue in federal court. In the same case, votes to deny access would be coded as promoting a liberal outcome, as they would have enabled the state's redistricting plan favoring minority voters to remain in place.

Table 12 displays the overall percentage of votes to grant access, as well as the percentage of votes cast in favor of access depending on whether the complaining party was pursuing a liberal or conservative cause. Differences in the values set forth in the second and third columns in Table 12 reflect the degree to which ideological factors shape the justices' voting behavior in these cases. Consider Justice Scalia, for example: he demonstrates an extreme commitment to judicial restraint when granting access would favor liberal causes, but is more than four times more likely to grant access when doing so

---

95. Whenever Spaeth had coded a substantive issue in connection with the case, we relied on his coding. When no substantive issue was coded, we coded each case in accordance with his coding conventions.

TABLE 12 Percentage of Votes to Grant Access to Federal Courts, Controlling for Ideological Direction of Substantive Outcome 1953–2004

Justice	Percentage Votes to Grant Access	Percentage Votes to Grant Access Where Outcome Would Be Liberal	Percentage Votes to Grant Access Where Outcome Would Be Conservative	Number of Votes
Black	62.69	70.33	25.00	67
Blackmun	45.59	46.22	43.33	136
Brennan	61.24	65.73	42.85	178
Breyer	39.29	35.00	50.00	28
Burger	19.19	12.34	50.00	99
Clark	50.00	61.29	11.11	40
Douglas	71.43	78.82	40.00	105
Frankfurter	29.63	27.77	33.33	27
Ginsburg	40.74	35.00	57.14	27
Harlan	33.90	33.33	36.36	59
Kennedy	35.09	22.50	64.70	57
Marshall	58.16	60.17	50.00	141
O'Connor	31.25	25.71	46.15	96
Powell	24.14	16.90	56.25	87
Rehnquist	24.36	15.96	70.37	156
Scalia	19.05	8.88	44.44	63
Souter	41.86	34.37	63.63	43
Stevens	56.41	57.30	53.57	117
Stewart	31.93	29.12	50.00	119
Thomas	23.68	7.40	63.63	38
Warren	64.91	78.26	20.00	57
White	45.93	42.14	62.50	172

would favor conservative litigants. Justice Rehnquist is more than five times more likely to grant access when it favors a conservative outcome, as is Justice Thomas. A similar pattern is evident in the voting behavior of Justice Kennedy, although he is far more likely in general to grant access.

The liberal justices also demonstrate ideological patterns in their voting behavior, but those patterns are far less pronounced: Justices Marshall, Brennan, Warren, Douglas, and Clark were more likely to grant access to achieve a liberal outcome. But none approach the multiplier effect of Justice Rehnquist or Thomas, although Warren comes close. In contrast, modern Court liberals Breyer, Souter, and Ginsburg show a willingness to grant access even when it produces a conservative result. And Blackmun, White, Stevens, Harlan, and Frankfurter demonstrate an evenhanded, nonideological approach when voting on issues of justiciability.

As in previous chapters, to categorize the justices in terms of their relative activism in these cases, we constructed a rough taxonomy based on their voting behavior on matters of justiciability. To do so, we created two dimensions: **institutional activism** and **ideological activism.** The first dimension simply reflects the justice's general willingness to grant access to the federal courts—justices were ranked high on this dimension if they voted to grant access more than 40% of the time (with Breyer a close call on this metric). The second dimension reflects the extent to which their votes indicate an ideological commitment to a particular policy outcome—justices ranked high on this dimension if their voting for one ideological outcome or the other varied by at least a factor of two. Justices in the "high institutional/high ideological" activism category were thus very willing to grant access but did so more often when it satisfied their personal policy preferences. Justices in the "high institutional/high ideological" category voted to expand access regardless of ideological outcome. Justices in the "low institutional/high ideological" category restricted access but did so ideologically, while justices in the "low institutional/low ideological" category restricted access across the board. The justices in the latter category might be perceived as the most restraintist in their voting behavior.

The fairly stringent standards we use to identify ideological activism clearly place some justices in unexpected categories. Thus Justice Douglas is listed as a justice who favors access but is not particular ideological in his decision making. To be sure, his votes to grant access are strongly liberal, but he is nevertheless quite willing to grant access to conservative parties as

TABLE 13 Taxonomy of Judicial Behavior—Votes to Grant Access to the Federal Courts

Institutional Activism	Ideological Activism	
	High	*Low*
High	Warren	Marshall
	Black	Blackmun
	Clark	Stevens
		Brennan
		Souter
		White
		Douglas
		Ginsburg
Low	Thomas	Harlan
	Powell	Frankfurter
	Rehnquist	Breyer
	Scalia	O'Connor
	Burger	Stewart
	Kennedy	

well. The same can be said of Justices Marshall and Brennan. Perhaps these justices are willing to grant access even to conservative parties because they favor the precedent that might be established—a precedent that eventually might favor a liberal plaintiff as well. Justices such as Scalia and Thomas, however, would essentially close the courthouse door to liberal interests altogether, while giving conservative interests a reasonable probability of entry. Thus they more clearly qualify as ideological activists.

We note in closing that Justice White presents a bit of a puzzle. In earlier analyses, he was consistently ranked among the most restraintist justices. Here, however, he votes to grant access with a relatively high probability. Yet these two results are not necessarily incommensurate. In some standing cases, the issue involves whether Congress granted parties statutory standing to challenge a violation of federal law. If Justice White voted to affirm congressional grants of standing, his vote would be aligned with deference to Congress. This is indeed a restraintist position, but vis-à-vis Congress rather than the judiciary. Thus it is possible that Justice White's higher activism ranking here may actually reflect his interest not in institutional aggrandizement of the judiciary, but rather in deference to the legislature.

⁂ C. Conclusion

The constitutional requirement of a "case or controversy" has been considered one of the "most elementary maxims of [judicial] restraint" (Lamb 1984, 15). Alexander Bickel labeled justiciability standards "passive virtues" because they could reduce the likelihood that the Court would overstep its appropriate institutional boundaries and interfere with policy making by the elected branches (Bickel 1962, 169). When the justices lower the threshold for parties to enter federal court, they increase the scope of the Court's policy-making power. Thus the implications of justiciability decisions for judicial activism are clear: expanding access increases the potential for institutional aggrandizement.

Our analysis in this chapter revealed considerable variation among the justices in terms of their propensity to grant access to the federal courts and thus to expand the Court's policy-making potential. At the same time, however, we demonstrated that sometimes judicial restraint in pursuit of the "passive virtues" can mask strategic voting in the interests of a particular ideological outcome. Several justices exhibited such ideologically motivated behavior in these cases, particularly Justices Scalia, Thomas, and Rehnquist.

SEVEN

Overruling Supreme Court Precedents

THE FINAL FORM OF activism we evaluate involves the justices' votes to overturn precedents established by an earlier Court. Such overruling decisions expressly reject a prior doctrinal rule and set a new legal standard; for that reason they implicate values of interpretive stability discussed in Chapter 2. Because they reverse the direction of a legal policy and reflect the abandonment of stare decisis, the customary method by which the Court reaches decisions, they constitute one dimension in the multidimensional concept of judicial activism.

The Supreme Court relies on precedent extensively in justifying its decisions (Epstein and Knight 1996), citing to precedent far more often than to any other source of law. Well aware of this fact, litigants refer extensively to precedents to persuade the justices to rule in their favor. Nevertheless, stare decisis is not a strictly binding rule, but rather constitutes a norm of decision making that may be abandoned under certain circumstances. As Chief Justice Rehnquist declared, stare decisis is "not an inexorable command" but instead constitutes a "principle of policy."[96] Nevertheless, while precedent is not legally binding on the Court, "any departure from the doctrine of stare decisis demands special justification."[97] For this reason, and perhaps because following precedent promotes institutional legitimacy and the appearance of continuity in Court rulings, historically the justices have been reluctant to overrule precedent previously established by the Court (see Stone 1988, 70). This reluctance is evident from the data: through 2004, the justices have overruled only 208 precedents in 133 decisions (Gerhardt 2008, 9). Thus the Court has explicitly overruled fewer precedents than it has invalidated statutes throughout its history.

---

96. *Payne v. Tennessee*, 501 U.S. 808, 828 (1991) (quoting *Helvering v. Hallock*, 309 U.S. 106, 119 (1940)).

97. *Arizona v. Rumsey*, 467 U.S. 203, 212 (1984).

On the other hand, outright overruling is not the only option available to a Court dissatisfied with rules announced in previous cases. Relevant precedents might simply be ignored. Alternatively, the precedent might be reinterpreted or its meaning manipulated to the point that the original doctrinal standards are substantially weakened.[98] As Judge Easterbrook has observed, the "alternative to disavowing precedent is manipulating it" (Easterbrook 1987, 424). At the same time, manipulating precedents technically leave them in place for future resurrection by justices more favorably predisposed to their application. In contrast, an outright overruling "limits recalcitrant lower courts in ways that distinguishing it or even limiting it cannot do" (Segal and Howard 2001, 157).

Identifying situations in which the individual justices manipulate or ignore precedent is difficult to achieve empirically and may involve subjective judgments regarding whether a particular precedent has been limited or abandoned altogether. While some excellent research has explored these phenomena at the Court level using codes developed by Shepard's citation service (Hansford and Spriggs 2006), coding is more difficult at the level of the individual justice, as Shepard's does not record subsequent citation history for individual concurrences or dissents. For these reasons, in this chapter we focus our attention on judicial voting behavior to overrule precedent explicitly. Fortunately, these votes are clearly identified in the Justice-Centered U.S. Supreme Court Judicial Database developed by Harold Spaeth and Sara Benesh for the years 1953 to 2000.[99]

We thus explore the justices' willingness to abandon "interpretive stability" and vote to overrule existing precedent. This forms our baseline measure of activism in this context. In addition, however, we also evaluate whether votes to overrule are affected by the justices' policy preferences.

---

98. For example, Professor Gerhardt has identified 17 cases in which the court functionally overruled prior decisions, though the language of these decisions contained no such overruling (Gerhardt 2008, 35). In other cases, he found that "the Court claims that it is relying on a precedent in a decision, but mischaracterizes it with the effect, if not the purpose, of undermining it" (Gerhardt 2008, 39). Yet since these judgments are somewhat subjective, we rely instead on the Spaeth/Benesh database for information about votes to overrule precedent explicitly.

99. The Justice-Centered Databases are more limited than the original U.S. Supreme Court Judicial Database in that they do not extend beyond the 2000 term. Hence our analysis is similarly limited.

✻ A. The Standard: Overruling Precedent

The action of overruling precedent raises different theoretical issues in relation to judicial activism than does invalidating statutes or expanding Court access. These latter decisions implicate concerns about counter-majoritarian power and institutional aggrandizement. Eliminating existing precedent arguably does not interfere with the separation of powers, as it does not directly infringe on the powers exercised by the coordinate branches. Nor does it necessarily result in institutional aggrandizement, especially if overruling precedent undermines the judiciary's institutional legitimacy. Nevertheless, common law courts follow precedent in part because it provides the appearance of legal constraint: when judges render decisions based on rules previously established in case law, it suggests that they are not simply "legislating from the bench" but are operating within well-defined doctrinal constraints. For that reason, Ernie Young has stressed that "the authority of precedent is generally thought to be one of the most important institutional characteristics of judicial decision making," and the "power to disregard such precedents suggests a *legislative* [rather than a judicial] decision" (Young 2002, 1150). Bradley Canon thus considered "interpretive stability" an important feature of judicial activism and determined that the explicit overruling of a prior Court precedent was highly activist (Canon 1983).

The framers of the Constitution considered precedent to "derive from the nature of judicial power and intended that it would limit the judicial power delegated to the courts by Article III of the Constitution."[100] The binding nature of precedent is seen as a constraint on judicial power and hence a limitation on activist decision making. Nevertheless, because the reversal of a precedent does not involve overturning the actions of *other* branches of government, it may be viewed as a lesser form of judicial activism (Hartnett 2005, 557). Indeed, Justice Douglas dismissed reliance on precedent as letting "men long dead and unaware of the problems of the age" do the justices' "thinking" (Douglas 1949, 736).

Justices have been known to upbraid their colleagues for their activist disregard of relevant precedent. In one dissent, Justice Brennan labeled the majority's opinion a "conspicuous exercise in judicial activism—particularly

---

100. *Anastasoff v. United States*, 223 F.3d 898, 900 (8th Cir. 2000), *vacated as moot en banc*, 235 F.3d 1054 (8th Cir. 2000).

so since it takes the form of disregard of precedent scarcely a month old."[101] In his final dissent, Justice Marshall criticized a pattern of overrulings, declaiming that "[p]ower, not reason" was "the new currency of the Court's decision making."[102] On other occasions, however, the justices have relied centrally on the significance of precedent in *not* overruling a prior decision. Perhaps the most prominent of these was the concurrence in *Planned Parenthood v. Casey*,[103] explaining that the Court would not overturn *Roe v. Wade*.[104] Similarly, the Court recently reaffirmed the decision in *Miranda v. Arizona*[105] out of respect for its precedential impact.[106] This reaffirmance was joined by Justice Rehnquist, even though he was a frequent critic of the original ruling in *Miranda*.

Reliance on precedent may be motivated by the Court's desire to legitimate its authority. Lacking the power of the purse or sword, the Court's capital rests in large part on public perceptions of its institutional legitimacy. Adherence to precedent strengthens the "external credibility" of the Court (Schauer 1987, 600). Judge Easterbrook likewise stressed that stare decisis "enhances the power of the justices" (Easterbrook 1982, 817), while Justice Stevens declared that following precedent "obviously enhances the institutional strength of the judiciary" (Stevens 1983, 2).

On the other hand, some have even argued that respect for precedent may itself be activist. For example, Steven Calabresi has suggested that the Court's failure to overturn *Roe* "is the biggest single indicia of the continuing problem we face today from judicial activism" (Calabresi 2004, 577). Michael Stokes Paulsen argues that the Court's respect for precedent is invoked to insulate judicial activism. He argues that the Court's decision in *Planned Parenthood v. Casey* upholding *Roe*, which relied on stare decisis as a doctrine of restraint, "creates a far more powerful image of adherence to the legal task than did *Roe's* transparently legislative opinion creating constitutional abortion rights out of thin air and thin precedents" (Paulsen 2003, 1033). For Paulsen, constitutional provisions should be interpreted according to original meaning without regard for precedents that may be incorrectly decided.

---

101. *Engle v. Issac*, 456 U.S. 107, 137 (1982) (Brennan, J., dissenting).

102. *Payne v. Tennessee*, 501 U.S.808, 844 (Marshall, J., dissenting).

103. 505 U.S. 833, 854–855 (1992).

104. 410 U.S. 113 (1973).

105. 384 U.S. 436 (1966).

106. *Dickerson v. United States*, 530 U.S. 428 (2000).

Justice Thomas seems sympathetic to this view and may believe that "precedent *qua* precedent concerning constitutional law has no value at all" (see Goldstein 2007).

However, Paulsen's position is not commonly held. In general, respect for past precedents is considered restraintist. Tom Merrill has explicated this position, arguing that respect for precedent promotes judicial restraint rather than activism (Merrill 2005, 273). He characterizes judicial activism in terms of unpredictable judicial outcomes, and precedent bolsters predictability. Failure to follow precedent can disrupt an institutional settlement of disputed questions and leave the law in a state of uncertainty. Merrill suggests that innovations are best left to elected officials, a separation of powers argument in its own right. This is evident from international comparisons, Merrill argues, as courts in the United Kingdom, with their stronger adherence to precedent, are regarded as less activist than United States courts, while the Canadian courts' recent shift away from emphasizing precedent has produced greater judicial activism (Merrill 2005, 283). Most commentators agree, therefore, that the decision to disrupt existing precedent threatens the judiciary's institutional legitimacy and places the Court in a position of appearing to "legislate from the bench." Of course, some might prefer this form of activism if it counteracts what they perceive to be *existing* activist decisions, what one might call "activism against activism." As Judge Posner has noted, "a decision overruling *Marbury v. Madison* would be wild stuff but it would be self-restrained . . . because it would reduce the power of the federal courts vis-à-vis the other organs of government" (Posner 1996, 319–320). Yet such a perspective does not change the fact that the latter decision is itself activist—it simply changes the justification for abandoning stare decisis.

✳ B. Overruling Precedents over Time

Michael Gerhardt's recent book examines the history of overruling precedents. In the nineteenth century, such decisions were quite rare, as the Marshall Court reversed no precedents, the Taney Court reversed but a single prior decision, and the Chase Court saw only two reversals (Gerhardt 2008, 11). In contrast, the Warren Court reversed 32 prior decisions, a rate that increased with the Burger Court's overruling 76 precedents (Gerhardt 2008, 12). The greater frequency of reversals may in part be due to the simple fact that, as time passes, the corpus of decisions to be potentially reversed naturally grows. On the other hand, the trend might also be related to an increase in the incidence of judicial activism.

We begin our analysis of this dimension to judicial activism by considering the history of the Court's overruling behavior since 1953. Figure 17 presents a frequency distribution of the number of cases by Court term in which the Court formally altered existing precedent. The graph illustrates the relative infrequency with which the Court has done so over time, although during some terms the Court has been quite activist in this regard. The early Warren Court seemed somewhat reticent to overturn precedent, but picked up steam after 1962. The Burger Court's frequency of overrulings held fairly steady, with the 1975 term representing a peak term with nine such decisions. The early years of the Rehnquist Court reflect fairly frequent overrulings as well.

Although claims of Rehnquist Court activism have tended to focus on the invalidation of federal statutes, that Court has also been criticized for undermining prior liberal precedents. One commentator noted that the Rehnquist Court's "dismantling of the federal habeas corpus remedy for state prisoners is as fine an example of unrestrained judicial activism and lack of candor as anything the Warren Court ever did" (Wells 1994, 123). Critics of that Court have argued that its conservatives "have done little to promote precedential restraint as an institutional value" and that they are "willing to ignore even the most basic tenets of *stare decisis*" (W.P. Marshall 2002, 1235–1236). This charge is not new to the Rehnquist Court, however, as the Warren Court was

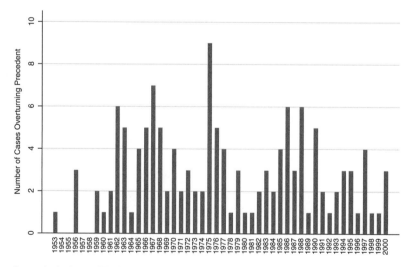

Source: Justice Centered Databases, alter_du variable, dec_type = 1, 2, 6, 7; analu = 0.

FIGURE 17 Frequency of Cases Formally Altering Precedent, by Court Term, 1953 to 2000

also charged with "casually overrul[ing] a great many criminal procedure precedents" (Vermeule 2005, 577). Justice Scalia claims that the Warren Court era was "marked by a newfound disregard for stare decisis."[107] Yet the data presented in Figure 17 suggest that the Rehnquist, Burger, and (later) Warren Courts were quite similar with respect to the formal alteration of precedent.

C. The Voting Behavior of the Individual Justices

1. The Frequency of the Justices' Votes to Formally Overrule Precedent

Although analysis of the Court's activity over time is useful, our objective is to assess the individual justices' respect for precedent. Several existing studies have evaluated the justices' voting behavior in relation to precedent and the choice to overrule. Lori Ringhand examined such actions for the recent Rehnquist Court (Ringhand 2007, 65). She found that conservative justices of the Court, especially Thomas and Scalia, were by far the most likely to vote to overturn an existing precedent. Gerhardt also analyzed these probabilities for the Rehnquist Court. He found that the number of annual justice-votes to reverse a precedent ranged from a high of 2.07 for Justice Thomas to a low of 1.0 for Justice Ginsburg (Gerhardt 2008).

To assess the frequency with which the individual justices voted to invalidate precedent, we relied on the U.S. Supreme Court Justice-Centered Databases, which record justice votes to invalidate an existing precedent, whether in majority, concurrence, or dissent. Figure 18 presents a dot plot reflecting the percentage of votes in all cases in which the individual justice voted to overrule precedent. To arrive at the percentage for each justice, the number of votes cast to overturn precedent (the numerator) is divided by the total number of votes cast by the justice throughout his or her career on the Warren, Rehnquist, or Burger Courts (the denominator).

The graph reveals the justices vote to formally overrule precedent infrequently and such votes for most of the justices cluster around 2%. Yet several current justices (Thomas, Scalia, and Kennedy) vote to overrule precedent at much higher rate, with Justices Scalia and Thomas voting to

---

107. *Harper v. Virginia Department of Taxation*, 509 U.S. 86, 108 (1993).

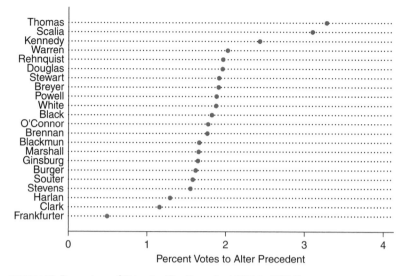

FIGURE 18 Percentage of Votes to Alter Precedent 1953 to 2000 Terms

overturn precedent in more than 3% of all cases in which they voted. Given how infrequently the Court overturns precedent, these figures reveal a distinct activism on the part of these justices in relation to precedent.

2. The Votes of the Individual Justices as Influenced by Ideology

Simple percentages do not reveal, however, whether the justices' votes to overrule precedent were motivated by their ideological disagreement with the existing precedent. Recent studies demonstrate quite convincingly, however, that these choices are often the product of the justices' policy preferences. The classic analysis that considered ideological activism was authored by Brenner and Spaeth (1995), who found that decisions to overrule precedent were largely driven by the justices' ideological preferences. Similarly, Ringhand found a strong ideological dimension to the justices' decisions to reverse a precedent. According to her recent study, liberal justices (Stevens, Ginsburg, Souter) did not vote to overturn a single liberal precedent during the period she studied (the Rehnquist Natural Court), while the most conservative justices (Thomas, Scalia) overturned liberal precedents at more than twice the rate they overturned conservative precedents (Ringhand 2007, 66). Segal and Howard studied cases decided between 1985 and 1994 in which the litigants requested that a precedent be reversed (Segal and Howard 2001). Although the sample size was limited, they found significant ideological disparities among the justices. Justice Rehnquist, for example, voted "to uphold precedents 71.4% of the time when conservative precedents [were] attacked, but only 36.7% of the time when liberal decisions [were] attacked" (Segal and Howard 2001, 157). They also found that the ideological influence was not uniform, however, as some justices, including Brennan, Stevens, and Souter, demonstrated support that "crossed ideological lines" (Segal and Howard 2001).

Spriggs and Hansford studied the overruling of Supreme Court precedent over a longer period (1946–1995), finding that the "ideological distance" between the median justice in the majority of the earlier cases and the median justice of the year of the overruling decision was a significant determinant of the decision to overrule (Spriggs and Hansford 2001, 1103). They also found that other variables, including some reflecting jurisprudential concerns, were also significant moderating factors. These included considerations such as whether the decision was statutory or constitutional, its treatment in intervening Supreme Court opinions, the size of the original majority coalition, and the case's legal complexity.

To assess the extent to which ideology shaped the justices' voting behavior in our sample, we calculated the proportion of cases in which the individual justices' vote to overrule existing precedent supported a liberal outcome. We contrast this figure with the liberalism of their overall voting behavior in cases that did not alter precedent. Table 14 presents these statistics.

The data presented in Table 14 reveal that nearly all the justices showed some ideological pattern in their votes to overturn precedent. Moreover, ideological voting tends to be more pronounced in situations in which the justices vote to overturn precedent, presumably because cases involving the overturning of precedent are more ideologically salient. Justice Breyer, for example, cast liberal votes about 55% of the time overall, but his votes to overturn precedent were liberal 83% of the time. Compare Justice Breyer's behavior with the results for Justice Thomas. He voted to alter precedent in a liberal direction only 26% of the time, indicating that his votes to overrule precedent were overwhelmingly conservative.

Based on these figures, we categorized the justices in terms of the frequency with which they voted to overturn precedent (which we label **institutional activism**), and the degree to which those votes were ideological, which we labeled **ideological activism**. This latter evaluation was based on the extent to which the justices deviated from an equal distribution

TABLE 14 Votes to Formally Alter Precedent, by Justice and Ideological Direction 1954–2000

Justice	Percent of Liberal Votes in Cases That Do Not Alter Precedent (Total N)	Percent of Liberal Votes in Cases That Alter Precedent (Total N)
Black	73% (2354)	98% (44)
Blackmun	52% (3488)	50% (60)
Brennan	70% (4986)	79% (91)
Breyer	55% (605)	83% (12)
Burger	34% (2635)	41% (44)
Clark	56% (1778)	67% (21)
Douglas	80% (2975)	95% (60)
Frankfurter	48% (997)	60% (5)
Ginsberg	56% (706)	83% (12)
Harlan	47% (2161)	69% (29)
Kennedy	41% (1388)	34% (45)
Marshall	72% (3474)	77% (60)
O'Connor	38% (2406)	23% (44)
Powell	39% (2323)	42% (45)
Rehnquist	29% (3896)	22% (79)
Scalia	35% (1602)	21% (52)
Souter	55% (1041)	65% (17)
Stevens	60% (3239)	63% (52)
Stewart	51% (3360)	62% (66)
Thomas	31% (904)	26% (31)
Warren	72%(2072)	93% (43)
White	49% (4607)	54% (89)

Source: Benesh/Spaeth Justice-Centered Databases. Cases selected using analu = 0; dec_type = 1, 2, 6, 7. Row percentages provided in parentheses, rounded up to nearest whole value. Ideological direction based on vt_dir variable.

of liberal and conservative votes. Where justices voted to invalidate precedent at about the same rate for liberal and conservative precedents (between 40% and 60% liberal), we coded them as ideologically neutral. Thus justices in the high institutional/high ideological activism category voted to invalidate precedent frequently and did so in an ideological fashion. Justices in the low institutional/high ideological category voted to overturn precedent infrequently, but did so in accordance with their policy preferences. Justices in the low institutional/low ideological category voted to invalidate infrequently and their votes were ideologically neutral when they did vote to overrule. No justice clearly fit within the high institutional/low ideological category, however.

The three justices whose voting behavior was most ideologically neutral when voting to overrule also voted to overrule very infrequently. For this

TABLE 15 Taxonomy of Judicial Behavior—Votes to Overturn Precedent

Institutional Activism	Ideological Activism	
	High	*Low*
High	Scalia	
	Thomas	
	Kennedy	
Low	Marshall	White
	Brennan	Blackmun
	Black	Frankfurter
	Douglas	Burger
	Warren	Powell
	Burger	
	Ginsberg	
	Rehnquist	
	Stevens	
	O'Connor	
	Souter	
	Ginsburg	
	Breyer	
	Harlan	

reason, Justices Blackmun, Frankfurter, and Burger fall into the low institutional/low ideological activism category. Because their voting behavior was so obviously different from that of the rest of the justices, only three justices were categorized as high institutional/high ideological: Justices Scalia, Kennedy, and Thomas.

🎗 D. Conclusion

According to our measures, contemporary conservatives lead the pack in terms of the form of activism associated with overturning precedents. Of course, given data constraints, this analysis is limited in that it only considers votes in which the individual justices make explicit their intent to overturn precedent. Some justices may be more underhanded in undermining precedents they disfavor. In that respect, one might argue that Justices Scalia, Thomas, and Kennedy act more forthrightly when they call for a precedent's invalidation. Yet to the extent institutional legitimacy turns on adherence to stare decisis, loud calls to overrule precedent may have potentially adverse effects on the judiciary as well. For that reason, votes to overturn precedent explicitly belong squarely in any analysis of judicial activism.

EIGHT

A Multidimensional View of Judicial Activism

IN CHAPTER 2, WE argued that judicial activism was best viewed as a multidimensional concept. Four theoretical constructs assisted us in identifying those dimensions: (1) counter-majoritarianism, (2) institutional aggrandizement, (3) interpretive stability and fidelity, and (4) result-oriented judging. In Chapters 3 through 5, we explored counter-majoritarianism by evaluating the justices' behavior in cases challenging the legality of state and federal legislation and federal administrative action. In Chapter 6, we considered institutional aggrandizement by exploring the justices' choices to expand access to the federal courts through lenient interpretations of justiciability doctrines. In Chapter 7, we evaluated the justices' adherence to principles of interpretive stability by considering their votes to overrule existing precedent. And across all these dimensions, we incorporated the extent to which the justices' policy preferences helped explain their voting behavior. Our analyses thus included the frequency with which the individual justices acted to invalidate governmental action, enhance judicial power, and disrupt precedential authority, as well as the justices' willingness to do so in accordance with their personal policy preferences.

Evaluating the dimensions individually has been illuminating. Certain justices stand out as particularly restraintist in the various contexts, including Byron White, Felix Frankfurter, and Warren Burger, while others are far more activist, including William Douglas, Clarence Thomas, and Thurgood Marshall. Yet without consolidating these individual measures into a composite appraisal, we will not have completed our task. To understand activism, we must formulate a comprehensive portrait of the justices based upon all the dimensions identified.

In this final chapter, therefore, we construct a composite measure of judicial activism, focusing on two dimensions distilled from the previous chapters. The first measure reflects the justices' levels of institutional activism. Here we include deference to the elected branches (Chapters 3 to 5), institutional modesty with respect to the judicial branch (Chapter 6), and deference to the precedents of previous Courts (Chapter 7). This dimension thus reflects justices' willingness to substitute their own judgments for those of other governmental actors, to expand judicial adjudicatory power, and to revise prevailing legal doctrines. Our second dimension, which we call ideological activism, reflects the justices' readiness to engage in these activities in furtherance of their own ideological preferences.

We make no normative judgments about whether activism is "bad" or "good." Caprice Roberts has criticized empirical analyses of judicial activism for embedding "flawed assumptions that such behavior is 'bad,' easily identifiable, and thus quantifiable" (Roberts 2007, 601). Perhaps this is sometimes true, but our analysis embeds no such assumptions. We do maintain that activism is at least somewhat identifiable and is thus quantifiable. But we also argue that activism is best seen as a simple descriptive measure, and not a normative one. Our primary focus is that activism which Judge Richard Posner characterized as a social-scientific one, in which "the Supreme Court is an object of observation rather than of veneration or condemnation" (Posner 2005, 32–33). Thus, for purposes of measurement, we make no normative assumptions. At the end of this chapter, however, we reflect on the normative debate in light of our empirical findings.

A. Dimensions of Judicial Activism

Our objective has been to identify dimensions of judicial activism that may be empirically measured, thus enabling us to compare Supreme Court justices who served during the Warren, Burger, and Rehnquist Courts. Evaluation of the justices' scores on these various measures allows us to draw some preliminary conclusions. First, some justices are far more deferential to legislative action than others. In particular, Rehnquist, Burger, Frankfurter, and White were generally deferential within both the state and federal contexts. Rehnquist, Burger, and White were also quite willing to defer to federal executive action. In terms of expansion of judicial authority in relation to doctrines of justiciability, again, we find Rehnquist, Burger, and Frankfurter exercising restraint by voting to grant access less often than many of their colleagues. As for interpretive stability, Frankfurter was the least likely to cast a vote to formally alter precedent, while Rehnquist was among the more activist justices in this regard.

Other justices were much less deferential to either legislators or executive officials. The voting behavior of Marshall, Brennan, Douglas, and Black demonstrated that they frequently voted to invalidate state and federal enactments, as well as federal administrative action. Warren was more deferential to Congress, but not to state governments or to the executive branch. Marshall, Brennan, Douglas, Black, and Warren were more likely to expand access to the federal courts as well.

As for ideological activism, several new names emerge. Among conservative justices, Thomas's, Scalia's, and Rehnquist's votes in cases challenging federal legislative and executive action showed an ideological orientation, as did their votes in matters relating to justiciability. Scalia and Thomas were somewhat less ideological in their voting behavior in cases challenging state legislation, but were quite ideological when it came to voting to overrule precedent. Some liberal justices also exhibited policy preference-motivated voting behavior in these cases, including Warren, Brennan, Douglas, and Black (with respect to federal and state legislation, as well as federal executive action), and Warren and Black (with respect to justiciability disputes).

1. Two-Dimensional Analysis

These findings suggest that certain justices "cluster" together when it comes to either institutional or ideological activism. To explore these dimensions further, we created a cumulative scale for each dimension. For the institutional activism scale, we simply added the percentages associated with each justice to (1) strike federal statutes, (2) strike state statutes, (3) strike federal administrative action, (4) grant access to the federal courts, and (5) overrule existing precedent.[108] Larger values on this scale indicate greater activism. For the ideological activism scale, we calculated the degree of ideological "skew" for each justice, whether it was the difference in likelihood between striking a liberal or conservative law or administrative action,[109] granting

---

108. In the case of precedent, the percentages were quite small—none exceeded 4%. This is because the percentage is based on a denominator that includes all votes cast by the individual justices and thus implicitly assumes that precedent is vulnerable to overruling in 100% of all cases. Because we regard this as highly unlikely, we multiplied this percentage by 10 on the assumption (albeit also somewhat arbitrary) that precedent is vulnerable to overruling in 10% of cases before the Court. Regardless of which value we used, however, the justices' rankings were the same.

109. In the case of administrative action, we calculated the difference between the justices' willingness to strike liberal action and 50%—a baseline standard midway between liberal and conservative behavior.

access to a liberal or conservative interest, or overruling a liberal or conservative precedent. Again, as values on this dimension increase, this measure indicates that the justices were increasingly motivated by ideology. A scatter plot reflecting the position of the justices on these two scales is presented in Figure 19.

The positions of the justices in Figure 19 reflect their relative degree of activism on the two dimensions. Justices clustered in the bottom left quadrant are the least activist on either dimension; those in the upper right, the most activist. Among the least activist justices are Frankfurter, White, Harlan, Burger, and Stewart. Blackmun also scores low on the ideological activism scale and is fairly restrained on institutional activism as well. Among the most activist justices are Douglas, Warren, Black, Brennan, Marshall, and, to a slightly lesser degree, Thomas. Several justices demonstrate institutional restraint, but are ideologically activist, including Rehnquist, Clark, and Scalia. Clustered in the middle are swing justices O'Connor and Kennedy, as well as Powell and Breyer.

What is to be made of these findings? First, the most interesting justices may be those who fall closer to the upper left or lower right quadrants. Justices in the upper left quadrant lean in the direction of institutional restraint, but their actions are otherwise significantly affected by their ideologies. Rehnquist and Clark fit into this category. Those closer to the lower

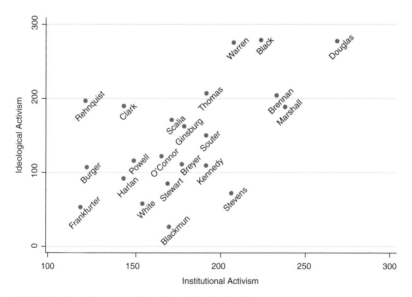

FIGURE 19 Two Dimensional Analysis of Judicial Activism

right quadrant are willing to intervene in the democratic process or expand judicial power, but are not particularly motivated by their policy preferences when taking those actions. Whether one or the other of these outcomes is preferable depends on one's perspective regarding the relative importance of the two dimensions. Those who prefer institutional modesty on the part of the judiciary may favor an approach that reduces judicial invalidation of actions by the elected branches or that reduces access to the courts, regardless of whether that institutional modesty is also shaped by the justices' policy views. Others may be willing to tolerate greater judicial intervention as long as it is achieved in an ideologically neutral fashion. These are normative judgments that we leave to our readers.

We also made one important assumption in creating these scales: we weighted each of the empirical measures equally. Thus votes to invalidate federal enactments, state enactments, administrative action, and so forth are all given equal weight. Alternative scales could be constructed that weight the composite measures differently, depending on whether one views certain elements of activism as more critical or important than others.

We also point out some apparent anomalies. Justice Blackmun demonstrates a very low level of ideological activism by our measure, as does Justice Stevens. As we have noted previously, these results could mask greater ideological decision making if the justices' behavior were analyzed at different periods in their careers. Agenda change could also have affected these results. Our presentation relies on career scores for these justices, however, and when viewed across the scope of their careers, any ideological variation over time may indeed be neutralized. Moreover, we note that the most restrained justice according to the two dimensions presented in Table 16 is Justice Frankfurter. While we believe the results are valid for the period of his service we analyze, they are based on a relatively small number of votes because he served on the Warren Court for only nine terms.

2. A Single Measure of Activism

Figure 19 presents a nuanced portrait of the justices' activism as it situates the justices in terms of their levels of both institutional and ideological activism. To produce a "final ranking" of activism, however, we also chose to construct a single scale that ranks these justices from least to most activist. Again, we relied on cumulative scaling techniques and simply cumulated their scores on both the institutional and ideological dimensions. Each element is scaled

TABLE 16 Cumulative Scale of Judicial Activism

Justice	Activism Score	Rank
Douglas	804	1
Black	709	2
Warren	672	3
Brennan	654	4
Marshall	649	5
Thomas	560	6
Souter	518	7
Ginsburg	503	8
Scalia	485	9
Stevens	470	10
Kennedy	469	11
Clark	465	12
Breyer	448	13
O'Connor	436	14
Rehnquist	419	15
Stewart	405	16
Powell	396	17
Harlan	365	18
Blackmun	350	19
White	348	20
Burger	334	21
Frankfurter	282	22

from 0 to 100, as they all constitute percentages. Each is weighted equally. We present these results in Table 16.

The results presented in Table 16 clearly track those in Figure 19. as they are based on the same constitutive elements. Here we see the Warren Court liberals ranked as the most activist, including Douglas, Black, Warren, Brennan, and Marshall. Conservative justice Clarence Thomas, however, is the next most activist justice by this measure, and Scalia is not far behind. The most restrained justices include Frankfurter, Burger, and White.

3. The Least Activist Justices

These cumulative scales and dimensional analysis confirm the common perception of Justice Frankfurter as a justice who practiced judicial restraint. Of course, as we've noted previously, Justice Frankfurter served on the Warren Court for only nine terms, so these data are somewhat limited. But at least for the period in which he served under Earl Warren, Frankfurter's voting behavior was consistent with his rhetorical commitment to judicial restraint (but see Spaeth 1964).[110] And it was during that period, of course, that he dissented in cases like *Baker v. Carr*[111] on grounds that reapportionment was a political question unfit for judicial resolution, and authored the majority opinion in *Poe v. Ullman*,[112] in which he wrote that plaintiffs lacked standing to challenge a Connecticut statute outlawing contraception. As Sandy Levinson has argued, this commitment to restraint was based on Frankfurter's fervent patriotism and dedication to American democracy. For Frankfurter, "[J]udicial restraint was a command of the American creed, and the function of the Supreme Court was limited to reminding the public that salvation could be attained only through individual initiative—and that the American polity would reward such initiative with political success. It is impossible to understand the intensity of Frankfurter's commitment to judicial restraint without comprehending the almost religious nature of his patriotism" (Levinson 1973, 447).

Warren Burger presents somewhat more of an enigma; according to one observer, his record on the Court "bedevils those who try to pigeonhole him" (Reske 1995). Moreover, little has been written about his jurisprudence. Anecdotally, Burger is known for participating in a number of liberal, activist decisions. He authored the opinion in *Reed v. Reed*,[113] the first decision by the Court finding arbitrary discrimination against women unconstitutional. He also voted to uphold court-ordered busing and to preserve the separation of church and state. On the federal side, in *Immigration and Naturalization Service v. Chadha*,[114] he struck down Congress's use of a legislative veto over actions by administrative agencies, a mechanism long used in federal statutes to control the bureaucracy, and ordered Richard Nixon to divulge the White House tapes. These decisions hardly reflect a jurist committed to institutional deference and restraint. Yet by our measures, he was otherwise very reticent to invalidate federal executive action, struck federal statutes very infrequently compared with his colleagues, and similarly had a low probability of voting to strike state action as well. As for access to the federal courts, he was second only to Scalia in terms of his unwillingness to find

---

110. Spaeth (1964) found that Justice Frankfurter's apparent restraint on labor cases masked a conservative orientation towards business interests.

111. 369 U.S. 186 (1962).

112. 367 U.S. 497 (1961).

113. 404 U.S. 71 (1971).

114. 462 U.S. 919 (1983).

plaintiffs' claims justiciable. It appears, then, that Warren Burger picked his battles carefully, generally exercising restraint except in cases involving highly salient issues. Indeed, some have claimed that "his votes in liberal rulings often were made in a desire to control the writing of an opinion rather than let it fall to Justice William Brennan" (Reske 1995, 36).

Justice White's restraint is somewhat less enigmatic. His "allegiance to Congress" is well-established in the literature (Powell Jr., et al. 1993, 25). Even his fellow justices have emphasized this characteristic. Justice Ginsburg suggested that he was activist in his votes to grant certiorari but "was in all other aspects of the Court's work a steadfast exemplar of the self-discipline often characterized as 'judicial restraint'" (Ginsburg 2003, 1285). Justice Stevens reported: "Of all the Justices with whom I have served, I remember Byron as the one who most consistently accorded a strong presumption of validity to the work of the Congress and the Executive" (Ginsburg 2003, 1285, quoting Justice Stevens). Perhaps alone among the justices of our era, Justice White broadly acknowledged the counter-majoritarian difficulty associated with the Court's rulings on the constitutionality of statutes (Bell 1999, 1380). As for precedent, "no member of the Court during his tenure was more committed to the doctrine of *stare decisis*,"[115] according to a resolution presented in his honor by members of the Supreme Court bar. White was also ecumenical in his devotion to legislative authority; when the Court turned more conservative, Justice White also resisted the efforts of the conservative justices, at least insofar as they restricted government authority (Tushnet 1998, 422). During that later conservative era, he opposed a series of federalism rulings that limited the federal government's powers.

Of course, Justice White was not entirely deferential, as he also joined some controversial activist holdings, such as finding a right to privacy in *Griswold*[116] and finding a right to travel in *Shapiro v. Thompson*.[117] He rendered a distinctly activist dissent in *San Antonio School District v. Rodriguez*,[118] in which the majority held that the Texas system for funding public education was valid under the Equal Protection Clause even though it produced a

115. Proceedings in the Supreme Court of the United States in Memory of Justice White, 537 U.S. v (2002). Available at http://law.onecle.com/ussc/justices/537usv-byron-white.html. Accessed December 26, 2008.

116. 381 U.S. 479 (1965).

117. 394 U.S. 618 (1969).

118. 411 U.S. 1 (1973).

wide disparity in revenue per student. Justice White would have struck the funding scheme on grounds that it denied equal protection to students in underfunded districts.[119] Nevertheless, we have shown that the overall pattern of his decision making was unusually deferential.

4. Assessing Restraint

The history of judicial activism described in Chapter 1 suggested that the practice is often criticized. During confirmation hearings, Supreme Court nominees are sometimes questioned pointedly about whether they would engage in activist decision making. Political rhetoric is rife with concerns over activist judging. Thus one might expect that justices who demonstrated considerable restraint would be among the most highly lauded jurists in Court history.

In this regard, we pause to consider the reputations of the three most restrained justices according to our measures, Justices Frankfurter, Burger, and White. Consider Justice White. Few have singled out White as among the most highly respected justices of the recent era. Instead, Justice White has been described as a "constitutional conservative who saw no major role for the Court in directing the course of the nation's social change" (Nelson 2003, 1297). White has also been contrasted with Justice Brennan, who "heroically tilted at windmills," while Justice White "in almost the same three-plus decades humbly bent in the direction of the wind" (Nelson 2003, 1299). These descriptions do not ring with high praise. The same could be said of Justice Burger. The portrait of Warren Burger painted in *The Brethren* hardly supports the view that he was a great Supreme Court justice (Woodward and Armstrong 1979). Even Frankfurter has been noted as having "disappointed many" in his career on the Court on grounds that his vision of a judiciary of "exceedingly limited powers" failed to adapt to a changing social environment (Shiffman 1992, 278-279, reviewing Urofsky 1991). Similarly, Mark Graber has criticized Frankfurter's restraint as a "false modesty" that failed to account for "crucial facts and underlying constitutional politics" (Graber 2007, 24).

A series of historians and lawyers have ranked the justices of the Supreme Court in terms of their quality. Frequently appearing on these "top 10" lists are activist Justices Warren, Brennan, and Black. Frankfurter occasionally appears as well, but not as frequently as Warren or Brennan. Justice White

---

119. 411 U.S. 1, 63-70 (1973).

and Burger never appear. The relative activists thus seem to be more highly regarded. Schwartz considered Justice Warren to be great because he "employed judicial authority to the utmost" and "never hesitated to do whatever he thought necessary to translate his conceptions of fairness and equality into the law of the land" (Schwartz 1997, 17). In short, Warren was considered great *because* he was a judicial activist. Thus, with respect to the *quality* of the restraintist justices in our study, commentary on "judicial greatness" does not suggest that they are the most highly rated.

On the other hand, simply because some justices consistently appear on "top 10" lists does not necessarily mean that other justices are not also praiseworthy, depending on one's perspective. If Schwartz and others placed activists on these lists because they approve of the substantive results reached by the highly rated justices (not to mention their willingness to use judicial power to achieve those results), their rankings simply constitute an embrace of policy-motivated judicial activism. That White saw "no major role for the Court in directing the course of the nation's social change" might be viewed quite favorably by those who believe the Court's role should be cabined in deference to democratic action. Moreover, what makes White and Frankfurter particularly compelling justices in this regard is that they pursued their constrained view of the proper judicial role without revealing much in the way of ideological leanings in doing so. Burger was somewhat more ideological, but even he was fairly constrained in this respect as well. One might argue that such neutrality is clearly worthy of recognition.

⚅ B. Evaluating Judicial Activism

To this point, our analysis of judicial activism has been largely descriptive. Given how prominent charges of judicial activism have become in public discourse, we believe it useful to bring some empirical rigor to the evaluation of judicial activism. We recognize, however, that it is the more normative evaluation of judicial activism that is central to the political debate. For that reason, we turn now to consider the normative issues in light of our empirical findings.

In the stereotypical ideological attack on judicial activism, activism is viewed monolithically and a "connotation of condemnation" is typically associated with the phrase (S.F. Smith 2002, 1079). Often, judicial activism is associated with the excessive exercise of judicial power in violation of principles of separated powers. Yet this should not simply be presumed. Perhaps some forms of judicial activism, neutrally defined, are a positive social good.

For example, Congress may adopt a law that is patently unconstitutional, in which case judicial decisions invalidating the statute would produce a positive outcome. Such a result does not usurp legislative authority so much as it defends the Constitution.

Ultimately, the "sin is not judicial activism, which may be warranted and healthy, but judicial activism bereft of persuasion and its crucial ingredients: reason, consistency, and principle" (Lazarus 1999, 517). Keenan Kmiec's excellent survey of judicial activism noted that "using 'activist' as a substitute for 'bad' elides important differences between the two labels; it fails to elucidate the specific ways in which a judicial opinion is improper, harmful, or wrong" (Kmiec 2004, 1473).

1. A Constrained Court

Judicial activism is therefore perhaps best assessed in terms of its practical impact on the common good. In this respect, Gerald Rosenberg's *The Hollow Hope* (1991) should be required reading for all critics of judicial activism. His work demonstrates that even the most socially progressive decisions by the Warren and Burger Courts, including *Brown v. Board of Education* and *Roe v. Wade*, had little actual impact *in themselves* in achieving the social change sought by the plaintiffs. His portrait is of a constrained Court whose rulings are often dependent on the political branches for effectuation. Indeed, judicial activism is not exercised in a vacuum. As we discussed at some length in Chapter 1, the Court operates within a system of separated powers and is itself subject to considerable constraints by the coordinate branches and by public opinion.

First, it is possible to undo judicially activist decisions through majoritarian action. Certainly, a constitutional ruling may be completely reversed only through amendment to the Constitution, an exceedingly difficult and time-consuming procedure. Other forms of activism are more readily overturned, however. If the Court reverses an administrative agency ruling as contrary to law, the Congress may simply amend the law to authorize such action. While this response may also prove difficult and imperfect, it can serve as an important constraint on judicial decisions, at least in the more extreme cases.

Congress may also alter the authority of the judiciary to make activist decisions, even those grounded in the Constitution. For example, Congress might pursue efforts to strip the Court of jurisdiction over certain kinds of disputes pursuant to Congress's legislative authority to determine federal court jurisdiction under Article III. Although some prominent commentators have suggested that this congressional power may be constitutionally limited, the Court has never so held, and the orthodox view is that the congressional power to alter federal court jurisdiction is broad. Although cases of jurisdiction stripping are fairly rare, the mere threat may intimidate the Court. After Supreme Court decisions in the 1950s restrained government action against subversive activity, a public backlash produced congressional efforts to strip jurisdiction. In response to this threat from Congress, the Court began "running away" from its earlier decisions "as fast as it could" (Powe 2000, 135), issuing new opinions limiting the scope of its earlier restrictions on the government.

One early empirical study of such Court-curbing activity found that the Court frequently retreated in response to legislative pressure (Nagel 1965). A subsequent study similarly concluded that after an increase in congressional proposals to strip the Court's power, the Court responded with decisions giving greater support to the government (Handberg and Hill Jr. 1980). Thus even mere threats from Congress may serve to curtail the Court. In addition to its power over jurisdiction, Congress also controls judicial resources, including judicial compensation (although this cannot be reduced, it may not be increased) and court budgets, and this tool appears to influence the Supreme Court as well (Cross and Nelson 2001, 1465–69, Toma 1991). Other forms of political pressure may also persuade the Court to reduce activist decision making. The infamous "switch in time that saved nine," reversing the *Lochner*-era pattern of Supreme Court decision making that invalidated early New Deal legislation, was arguably a product of such pressure.

Finally, several studies have shown that the Court's opinions are generally majoritarian in nature. Although the court seldom references public opinion as a basis for its rulings, researchers have found that the Court's decisions are usually consistent with it (Mishler and Sheehan 1993). Indeed, studies have found that the Court's rulings align with broad public opinion about as often as legislative action does (T. R. Marshall 1989, 80).

An example of effective congressional response to judicial activism can be found in relation to federal courts' active monitoring of prison systems on grounds that prison conditions were violating prisoners' constitutional and statutory rights (U.S. Senate 1997, 11). Eventually, members of Congress came to believe that judicial intervention in the management of prison systems had become too intrusive. In response, Congress used its authority to restrain the judiciary through jurisdictional limitations. The Prison Litigation Reform Act[120] was passed in order to limit the ability of federal courts to impose certain remedial decrees on prisons. The Anti-Terrorism and Effective Death Penalty Act[121] restricted the ability of state prisoners to file habeas corpus petitions in federal court. These actions were generally viewed as a "response to undue 'judicial activism'" (Jackson 1998, 2448) and demonstrate the ability of the elected branches to restrain perceived judicial activism, even when such activism is constitutionally grounded.

The prison litigation episode implicitly reveals the many "dogs that didn't bark," however. The vast bulk of activist decisions have gone unchallenged by Congress. In some cases, the legislature has considered constraints on judicial activism, but backed away. After the *Brown* decision, Congress considered withdrawing the Court's jurisdiction to hear school desegregation cases, and the legislature soon thereafter considered similar action in cases involving investigation of subversive activities (Eisenberg 1974, 498–499). These efforts failed. By the 1980s, Congress was proposing numerous jurisdiction-stripping statutes related to issues such as prayer in schools, abortion, and busing as a remedy to desegregation, but took no action (Tribe 1981, 136–139). Whether because of difficulties inherent in enacting legislation, or simply because the issues were insufficiently compelling to warrant legislative action, these examples indicate that in many cases, congressional inaction enables activist decisions to remain in place.

As we saw in Chapter 1, the political response to claimed excesses of judicial activism has often been most pronounced in connection with the appointment of new Supreme Court justices. Nixon's Burger Court and Reagan's Rehnquist Court were both purportedly formulated to unravel the judicial activism of the Warren Court, but neither had much effect in this regard. The Burger Court's decisions have been regarded as a slowing, but certainly not a reversal, of Warren Court activism. Despite "the enormous controversy that resulted from the Warren Court's work, the survival and acceptance of the fundamental doctrinal developments of the Warren Court era result from its largely successful effort to accommodate a newly developing pattern of pluralism in America" (F.P. Lewis 1999, 3). Indeed, the Burger

---

120. Prison Litigation Reform Act of 1995, Pub. L. No. 104-134, 110 Stat. 1321 (codified as amended in scattered titles and sections of the U.S.C.).

121. Anti-Terrorism and Effective Death Penalty Act of 1996, Pub. L. No. 104-132, 110 Stat. 1214 (codified as amended in scattered titles and sections of the U.S.C.).

and Rehnquist Courts built substantially on the Warren Court's *Griswold* legacy, with activist decisions such as *Roe v. Wade*[122] and *Lawrence v. Texas*.[123] The Burger Court further extended the Warren Court legacy in granting equal protection rights based on gender. Moreover, the defeat of Robert Bork's nomination to the Supreme Court has been seen as an affirmation of the virtues of liberal judicial activism (Wolfe 1997, 54). Conservatives "feel that the Left rode out the Reagan/Bush (senior) years without losing a single major activist precedent" (Calabresi 2004, 579).

2. A Moral Good?

Our results have shown that the justices of the Warren Court were especially activist in several dimensions. Yet one could easily argue that "[m]odern judicial activism, particularly that of the Court under Chief Justice Warren, was a desirable development" (A.S. Miller 1982, 9). Few today question the value of *Brown v. Board of Education* and its declaration of governmental racial neutrality has been widely embraced by conservatives. The Warren Court's decisions on behalf of free speech rights have been adopted and expanded subsequently by both conservative and liberal justices. The fact that "the tolerant libertarian view of the free speech clause has such broad support in contemporary America and on a Court that has become increasingly conservative is yet another example of Warren Court activism moving doctrine in a direction that has both persisted and further developed" (F.P. Lewis 1999, 38). Although some of its decisions on behalf of criminal defendants' rights remain more controversial, many basic holdings such as the right to counsel for indigents established in *Gideon v. Wainwright*[124] are generally embraced today. The reapportionment holding in *Reynolds v. Sims*[125] was regarded as very activist at the time, but few today challenge its principle of "one man, one vote." Indeed, this decision ultimately provided the Court "with enhanced power and popular prestige" (Wolfe 1997, 53).

One might also consider the 1967 decision in *Katz v. United States*.[126] Forty years earlier, the Supreme Court had held that a wiretap interception of

---

122. 410 U.S. 113 (1973).

123. 539 U.S. 558 (2003).

124. 372 U.S. 335 (1963).

125. 377 U.S. 533 (1964).

126. 389 U.S. 347 (1967).

a private telephone call was not a "search" under the Fourth Amendment, as there was no physical intrusion into the person's home.[127] In *Katz*, the Court rejected that approach, a decision that was activist in both vacating a conviction on constitutional grounds and reversing a Supreme Court precedent. The Court held that the Fourth Amendment should be interpreted to provide greater protection of personal privacy. Although *Katz* has been labeled as an activist "legislative decision" that "disregarded the Fourth Amendment's words and original purpose in order to bring a novel form of criminal investigation under the Constitution" (Posner 2008a, 201), we nevertheless suspect that few Americans object to the decision in *Katz* today.

While commentators often defend the Court's liberal activism, conservatives have made similar claims in regard to conservative activism. In connection with the Fourth Circuit decision striking the Violence against Women Act, Judge Wilkinson declared that the "decision will assuredly be characterized as unjustifiable activism," but "just as assuredly, that characterization will miss the mark."[128] Rather, he asserted, the decision "vindicates the role of the judiciary" in its enforcement of the "concept of enumerated powers" found in the Constitution.[129] The more recent conservative activism has not yet had the opportunity to obtain the historical pedigree by which at least some of the Warren Court's liberal activism has been politically validated. Yet this surely remains a possibility, as today's conservative activism may become accepted, settled law. Over time, the Court may produce a renaissance of federalism and restriction of federal government authority viewed as beneficial by society. Conversely, if the recent conservative decisions are subsequently disapproved, they may fall by the wayside of constitutional jurisprudence, just as the *Lochner*-era rulings did.

It is also noteworthy that some of the Court's most lamented decisions have been produced by the exercise of restraint. One of the more deferential decisions in history, *Korematsu v. United States*,[130] upheld an Executive Order requiring that Japanese-Americans on the West Coast be interned in relocation camps. Justice Frank Murphy dissented, characterizing the action as racist, as did Justice Robert Jackson, who feared the future effect of the

---

127. *Olmstead v. United States*, 277 U.S. 438 (1928)

128. *Brzonkala v. Va. Polytechnic Inst. & State Univ.*, 169 F.3d 820, 897 (Wilkinson, J., concurring).

129. *Id.*

130. 323 U.S. 214 (1944).

precedent. While the dissenters were the activists in *Korematsu*, they are today regarded as the justices who correctly championed constitutional principles in the face of oppressive governmental power. In 1988, the U.S. Congress apologized for the internment, describing it as a "grave injustice."[131]

Similarly, observers have criticized the Court's failure to invalidate the Sedition Act in the early days of the Republic (U.S. Senate 1997, 26 (statement of Bruce Fein)), yet it represented a position of judicial restraint. The Supreme Court's limited interpretation of the Civil War Amendments to the Constitution in decisions such as the *Slaughter-House Cases*[132] and the *Civil Rights Cases*,[133] significantly undermined the ends of those constitutional amendments. Surely, a Court that always ruled for the government or that refused to even hear any cases challenging the government's actions would be a paragon of restraint, but that Court would be regarded as one that had abdicated its constitutional duties. A measure of judicial independence from the elected branches is a key element of our constitutional structure.

Of course, some activist decisions are also greatly lamented. The historical jury is still out on some of the more recent activist rulings, but *Dred Scott v. Sanford*,[134] which invalidated the Missouri Compromise, is certainly considered an unfortunate example of activist decision making.

The foregoing discussion suggests that even the most activist decisions are rendered in a political environment where they are subject to acceptance, disapproval, and even reversal, but that often decisions considered activist at the time they are rendered come to gain social and political acceptance. That is not to say that some activist decisions do not continue to generate considerable controversy in the political arena; *Roe v. Wade* is the obvious case. But the extent of the continuing dialogue over *Roe*, as well as the successful efforts by many states to limit abortion rights even after *Roe*, indicates that activist decisions like *Roe* do not completely stifle democratic action and debate. The Court rarely has the last word.

Thus analysis of activism cannot end with the consideration of the Court's decisions alone. Political scientists have made great strides in evaluating the

---

131. Civil Liberties Act of 1988, "Restitution for World War II Internment of Japanese-Americans and Aleuts," 50 App. U.S.C.A. § 1989 (West 2008).

132. 83 U.S. 36 (1873).

133. 109 U.S. 3 (1883).

134. 60 U.S. 393 (1856).

actual impact of the Court's decisions, as well as the extent to which the Court's judgments are constrained by its political environment. Moreover, as this study has shown, activism must also be evaluated in terms of how often activist decisions are rendered in a result-oriented fashion. Where the justices engage in activist decision making in a manner that systematically advances their policy preferences, and exercise restraint in the same fashion, their behavior supports the jaundiced view of a political Court. Exposing these patterns to public scrutiny may serve as a cautionary note to decision makers as they consider the implications of their actions over multiple cases and multiple votes. Indeed, rationalizing a single decision may prove persuasive at the level of individual case analysis. But studies that reveal patterns of behavior across many cases more effectively reveal which justices practice result-oriented activism on a broader scale.

✎ C. The Contribution of Empirical Research

In this study we have sought to shed some light on debates over judicial activism by studying the individual justices' behaviors empirically and systematically along several different dimensions. Our objective has been to move away from anecdotal or historical accounts focusing on individual cases or groups of cases, to evaluate the full scope and impact of each justice's behavior across many decisions and issue areas. By employing a multidimensional approach, we have sought to avoid the pitfall of viewing activism through a single lens.

To be sure, our findings may not change minds about the benefits and costs of judicial activism; nor was that our objective. But they do suggest that justices are not monolithic in their methods of decision making; some justices are more activist in some areas than in others. And perhaps the most laudable justices are those who resist the temptation to render decisions in a predictable ideological direction. Our portrait of the justices' behavior therefore enables a more nuanced view of the concept beyond mere name-calling. In identifying and quantifying measures of judicial activism, we hope to have moved the discussion forward in a way that elevates the term from simple epithet to meaningful concept.

References

Abraham, Henry. 1992. *Justices and Presidents* 3rd ed. New York: Oxford University Press.

Allan, T. R. S. 2003. *Constitutional Justice: A Liberal Theory of the Rule of Law.* New York: Oxford University Press.

Anderson, Jeffrey H. 2006. Learning from the Great Council of Revision Debate. *Review of Politics* 68(1): 79–100.

The Asia Foundation. 2003. Report to the Asian Development Bank, Judicial Independence: Overview and Country-Level Summaries. http://www.adb.org/Documents/Events/2003/RETA5987/Final_Overview_Report.pdf (accessed September 30, 2008).

Atkins, Burton, and William Taggart. 1984. Substantive Access Doctrines and Conflict Management in the Supreme Court: Reflections on Activism and Restraint. In *Supreme Court Activism and Restraint*, ed. Stephen C. Halpern and Charles M. Lamb, 351-384. Lexington, MA: Lexington Books.

Balkin, Jack. M., and Sanford Levinson. 2001. Understanding the Constitutional Revolution. *Virginia Law Review* 87: 1045–1109.

Balla, Steven J., and John R. Wright. 2001. Interest Groups, Advisory Committees, and Congressional Control of the Bureaucracy. *American Journal of Political Science* 45(4): 799–812.

Barak, Aharon. 1989. *Judicial Discretion.* New Haven: Yale University Press.

Barber, Sotorios A. 1988. Judicial Review and "The Federalist." *The University of Chicago Law Review* 55(3): 836–887.

Barnett, Randy. 1987. Judicial Activism is Necessary. *Legal Times*, April 27.

Barnum, David G. 1985. The Supreme Court and Public Opinion: Judicial Decision Making in the Post-New Deal Period. *The Journal of Politics* 47(1): 652–666.

Baum, Lawrence. 1987. Explaining the Burger Court's Support for Civil Liberties. *PS* 20: 21–28.

Baum, Lawrence. 2006. *Judges and Their Audiences.* Princeton: Princeton University Press.

Belknap, Michael. 2005. *The Supreme Court under Earl Warren, 1953-1969.* Columbia, SC: University of South Carolina Press.

Bell, Bernard W. 1999. Byron R. White, Kennedy Justice. *Stanford Law Review* 51(5): 1373–1476.

Bell, Bernard W. 2003. Judging in Interesting Times: The Free Speech Clause Jurisprudence of Justice Byron R. White. *Catholic University Law Review* 52(4): 893–914.

Benesh, Sara, and Harold Spaeth. 2005. The Justice-Centered United States Supreme Court Judicial Databases. AnnArbor, MI: Inter-University Consortium for Social and Political Research. Available at http://www.cas.sc.edu/poli/juri/.

Berger, Raoul. 1977. *Government by Judiciary: The Transformation of the Fourteenth Amendment.* Cambridge: Harvard University Press.

Beth, Loren P. 1961. The Supreme Court and the Future of Judicial Review. *Political Science Quarterly* 76(1): 11–23.

Bickel, Alexander M. 1961. Foreword: The Passive Virtues. *Harvard Law Review* 75(1): 40–79.

Bickel, Alexander M. 1962. *The Least Dangerous Branch: The Supreme Court at the Bar of Politics.* Indianapolis: Bobbs-Merrill.

Bickel, Alexander M. 1986. *The Least Dangerous Branch: The Supreme Court at the Bar of Politics.* 2nd ed. New Haven: Yale University Press.

Blasi, Vincent, ed. 1986. *The Burger Court: The Counter-Revolution That Wasn't.* New Haven: Yale University Press.

Blaustein, Albert P., and Roy Mersky. 1972. Rating Supreme Court Justices. *ABA Journal* 58(11): 1183–1188.

Bolick, Clint. 2007. A Cheer for Judicial Activism. *Wall Street Journal*, April 3.

Bolick, Clint. 2007. *David's Hammer: The Case for an Activist Judiciary.* Washington, D.C.: Cato Institute.

Bork, Robert. 1990. At Last, an End to Supreme Court Activism. *New York Times*, August 29.

Bradley, Robert C. 2003. Selecting and Ranking Great Justices: Poll Results. In *Leaders of the Pack: Polls and Case Studies of Great Supreme Court Justices,* ed. William D. Pederson and Norman W. Provizer, 1-22. New York: Peter Lang Publishing.

Brenner, Saul, and Harold Spaeth. 1995. *Stare Indecisis: The Alteration of Precedent on the Supreme Court, 1946–1992.* Cambridge: Cambridge University Press.

Breyer, Stephen. 2005. *Active Liberty: Interpreting Our Democratic Constitution.* New York: Knopf Publishing Group.

Brown, Rebecca L. 2002. Activism Is Not a Four-Letter Word. *University of Colorado Law Review* 73(4): 1257–1274.

Bush, George W. 2001. Remarks Announcing Nominations for the Federal Judiciary. *Weekly Compilation Of Presidential Documents* (May 9) 37: 724–725.

Bush, George W. 2003. Prime Time Special Event (December 16). Interview by Diane Sawyer. ABC News.

Bush, George W. 2006. State of the Union Address (January 31). http://www.whitehouse.gov/stateoftheunion/2006/index.html. (accessed June 2008).

Calabresi, Steven G. 2004. The Congressional Roots of Judicial Activism. *Journal of Law and Politics* 20: 577–593.

Calabresi, Steven G., and Gary Lawson. 2007. The Unitary Executive, Jurisdiction Stripping, and the *Hamdan* Opinions: A Textualist Response to Justice Scalia. *Columbia Law Review* 107(4): 1002–1047.

Calabresi, Steven G., and Christopher S. Yoo. 1997. The Unitary Executive during the First Half-Century. *Case Western Reserve Law Review* 47: 1452–1561.

Caldeira, Gregory A. 1986. Neither the Purse nor the Sword: Dynamics of Public Confidence in the Supreme Court. *American Political Science Review* 80: 1209–1226.

Caldeira, Gregory A. 1987. Public Opinion and the U.S. Supreme Court: FDR's Court-Packing Plan. *American Political Science Review* 81(4): 1139–1153.

Caminker, Evan H. 2003. Thayerian Deference to Congress and Supreme Court Supermajority Rule: Lessons from the Past. *Indiana Law Journal* 78(1): 73–122.

Canon, Bradley C. 1983. Defining the Dimensions of Judicial Activism. *Judicature* 66: 237–247.

Canon, Bradley C. 1984. A Framework for the Analysis of Judicial Activism. In *Supreme Court Activism and Restraint*, ed. Stephen C. Halpern and Charles M. Lamb, 385–419. Lexington: Lexington Books.

Canon, Bradley C., and Michael Giles. 1972. Recurring Litigants: Federal Agencies before the Supreme Court. *Western Political Quarterly* 25: 183–191.

Casper, Jonathan. 1976. The Supreme Court and National Policy Making. *American Political Science Review* 70: 50–63.

Chae, Young-geun. 2000. The U.S. Supreme Court's Policy Preference and Institutional Restraint in Environmental Law. *Wisconsin Environmental Law Journal* 7(1): 41–92.

Chemerinsky, Erwin. 2000. Perspective on Justice. *Los Angeles Times*, May 18.

Chemerinsky, Erwin.2002. The Rhetoric of Constitutional Law. *Michigan Law Review* 100(8): 2008–2035.

Choper, Jesse. 1983. *Judicial Review and the National Political Process*. Chicago: University of Chicago Press.

Clarke, Wes. 1997. Budget Requests and Agency Head Selection Methods. *Political Research Quarterly* 50(2): 301–316.

Clinton, William Jefferson. 2000. Remarks at a People for the American Way Reception. *Weekly Compilation Of Presidential Documents* (October 30) 36: 2610.

Clayton, Cornell W. 1994. Separate Branches, Separate Politics: Judicial Enforcement of Congressional Intent. *Political Science Quarterly* 109(5): 843–873.

Cohen, Adam. 2005. Is John Roberts Too Much of a Judicial Activist? *New York Times*, August 27.

Cohen, Adam. 2006. What Chief Justice Roberts Forgot in His First Term: Judicial Modesty. *New York Times*, July 9.

Cohen, Adam. 2007. Last Term's Winner at the Supreme Court: Judicial Activism. *New York Times*, July 9.

Cohen, Linda R., and Matthew L. Spitzer 1994. Solving the Chevron Puzzle. *Law and Contemporary Problems* 57(2): 65–110.

Cohn, Margit, and Mordechai Kremnitzer. 2005. Judicial Activism: A Multidimensional Model. *Canadian Journal of Law and Jurisprudence* 18(2): 333–356.

Comiskey, Michael. 2004. *Seeking Justices: The Judging of Supreme Court Nominees*. Lawrence: University Press of Kansas.

Congressional Research Service. 2005. *The Supreme Court's Overruling of Constitutional Precedent: An Overview*. Washington D.C.: CRS.

Cordray, Margaret M., and Richard Cordray. 2001. The Supreme Court's Plenary Docket. *Washington and Lee Law Review* 58: 737–794.

Cross, Frank B. 1997. Political Science and the New Legal Realism: A Case of Unfortunate Interdisciplinary Ignorance. *Northwestern University Law Review* 92(1): 251–326.

Cross, Frank B. 1999. Shattering the Fragile Case for Judicial Review of Rulemaking. *Virginia Law Review* 85(7): 1243–1334.

Cross, Frank B. 2000. Institutions and Enforcement of the Bill of Rights. *Cornell Law Review* 85: 1529–1608.

Cross, Frank B. 2007. *Decision Making in the U.S. Courts of Appeals.* Stanford, CA: Stanford University Press.

Cross, Frank B., and Blake Nelson. 2000. Strategic Institutional Effects on Supreme Court Decisionmaking. *Northwestern University Law Review* 95(4): 1437–1494.

Cross, Frank B., and Stefanie A. Lindquist. 2006. The Decisional Significance of the Chief Justice. *The University of Pennsylvania Law Review* 154: 1665–1707.

Crovitz, L. Gordon, and Jeremy Rabkin. 1989. *The Fettered Presidency.* Washington, D.C.: American Enterprise Institute.

Crowley, Donald W. 1987. Judicial Review of Administrative Agencies: Does the Type of Agency Matter? *The Western Political Quarterly* 40(2): 265–283.

Cushman, Barry. 1998. *Rethinking the New Deal Court: The Structure of a Constitutional Revolution.* New York: Oxford University Press.

Dahl, Robert A. 1957. Decision-Making in a Democracy: The Supreme Court as National Policy Maker. *Journal of Public Law* 6: 279–295.

Deen, Rebecca E., James Ignagni, and James Meernik. 2005. Rehnquist Court and Support of Federal Agencies. *Judicature* 89(3): 154–160.

Dinan, John. 2004. Strengthening the Political Safeguards of Federalism: The Fate of Recent Federalism Legislation in the U.S. Congress. *Publius: The Journal of Federalism.* 34: 55–84.

Dionne, E. J. 2007. Verdict Is In: Activism Rules Roberts Court. *Investors Business Daily,* June 28.

Douglas, William O. 1949. Stare Decisis. *Columbia Law Review* 49(6): 735–758.

Dow, David R., Cassandra Jeu, and Anthony C. Coveny. 2008. Judicial Activism on the Rehnquist Court: An Empirical Assessment. *St. John's Journal of Legal Commentary.* 23: 35–110.

Durant, Robert F. 1992. *The Administrative Presidency Revisited: Public Lands, the BLM, and the Reagan Revolution.* Albany: State University of New York Press.

Durr, Robert H., Andrew D. Martin, and Christina Wolbrecht. 2000. Ideological Divergence and Public Support for the Supreme Court. *American Journal of Political Science* 44(4): 768–776.

Easterbrook, Frank H. 1982. Ways of Criticizing the Court. *Harvard Law Review* 95(4): 802–832

Easterbrook. 1987. Stability and Reliability in Judicial Decisions. *Cornell Law Review* 73(2): 422–433.

Easterbrook. 1990. Presidential Review. *Case Western Reserve Law Review* 40(4): 905–929.

Easterbrook. 2002. Do Liberals and Conservatives Differ in Judicial Activism? *University of Colorado Law Review* 73(4): 1403–1416.

Edelman, Paul, David E. Klein, and Stefanie A. Lindquist. 2008. Measuring Deviations from Expected Voting Patterns on Collegial Courts. *Journal of Empirical Legal Studies* 5(4): 821–854.

Egelko, Bob. 2004. Brown v. Board of Education: 50 Years Later 1954 Ruling Seen as Model of Judicial Activism. *San Francisco Chronicle*, May 17.

Eisenberg, Theodore. 1974. Congressional Authority to Restrict Lower Federal Court Jurisdiction. *Yale Law Journal* 83(3): 498–533.

Ely, John Hart. 1980. *Democracy and Distrust: A Theory of Judicial Review.* Cambridge: Harvard University Press.

Engel, Stephen M. 2007. Attacking the Court: A Theory of Political Contingency and Initial Findings Drawn from National Party Platforms. Paper presented at the Midwest Political Science Association Annual Meeting, April 12, in Chicago, IL.

Epstein, Lee, and Jack Knight. 1996. The Norm of Stare Decisis. *American Journal of Political Science* 40(4): 1018–1035.

Epstein, Lee, Andrew D. Martin, Kevin M. Quinn, and Jeffrey A. Segal. 2007. Ideological Drift Among Supreme Court Justices: Who, When, and How Important? *Northwestern University Law Review* 101: 1483–1542.

Epstein, Richard A. 2007. Scalia's Judicial Activism. *Wall Street Journal*, June 29.

Feeley, Malcolm M., and Edward L. Rubin. 1998. *Judicial Policy Making and the Modern State: How the Courts Reformed America's Prisons.* Cambridge: Cambridge University Press.

Fowler, James H., Timothy R. Johnson, James F. Spriggs II, Sangick Jeon, and Paul J. Wahlbeck. 2007. Network Analysis and the Law: Measuring the Legal Importance of Precedents at the U.S. Supreme Court. *Political Analysis* 15: 324–346.

Friedman, Barry. 1993. Dialogue and Judicial Review. *Michigan Law Review* 91(4): 577–682.

Friedman, Barry. 2002. The Birth of an Academic Obsession: The History of the Countermajoritarian Difficulty, Part Five. *Yale Law Journal* 112(2): 153–259.

Furlong, Scott. 1998. Political Influence on the Bureaucracy: The Bureaucracy Speaks. *Journal of Public Administration Research and Theory* 8(1): 39–65.

Garland, Merrick. 1985. Deregulation and Judicial Review. *Harvard Law Review* 98(3): 505–591.

Garner, Bryan. 2004. *Black's Law Dictionary.* 8th ed. St. Paul, MN: West Group.

Garnett, Richard W. 2007. The Virtue of Humility. *University of Pennsylvania Law Review* 155: 112–128.

Gates, John B. 1987. Partisan Realignments, Unconstitutional State Policies, and the. U.S. Supreme Court. *American Journal of Political Science* 31: 259–80.

George, Joyce J. 2000. *Judicial Opinion Writing Handbook.* 4th ed. New York: William S. Hein Publishing.

Gerhardt, Michael. 2008. *The Power of Precedent.* New York: Oxford University Press.

Gewirtz, Paul, and Chad Golder. 2005. So Who Are the Activists? *New York Times*, July 6.

Gillman, Howard. 1993. *The Constitution Besieged: The Rise and Demise of Lochner Era Police Powers Jurisprudence.* Durham, NC: Duke University Press.

Ginsburg, Ruth Bader. 2003. Remembering Justice White. *University of Colorado Law Review* 74(4): 1283–1290.

Goldstein, Thomas C. 2007. Justice Thomas: Constitutional "Stare Indecisis." First Amendment Center Online: Symposium on Justice Thomas and the First Amendment. Available at http://www.firstamendmentcenter.org/analysis.aspx?id=19133 (accessed December 8, 2008).

Graber, Mark. 2007. False Modesty: Justice Frankfurter and the Tradition of Judicial Restraint. *Washburn Law Journal* 47: 23–34.

Graglia, Lino A. 1976. *Disaster by Decree: The Supreme Court Decisions on Race and the Schools.* Ithaca, NY: Cornell University Press.

Greenhouse, Linda. 2005. The Court v. Congress. *New York Times*, September 15.

Greenhouse, Linda. 2006. *Becoming Justice Blackmun: Harry Blackmun's Supreme Court Journey.* New York: Times Books.

Hamilton, Alexander. 1788. The Federalist 78: A View of the Constitution of the Judicial Department in Relation to the Tenure of Good Behaviour. In *James Madison, Alexander Hamilton and John Jay, The Federalist Papers,* ed. Isaac Kramnick, 436-441. New York: Penguin Books.

Handberg, Roger. 1976. The Supreme Court and Administrative Agencies: 1965–1978. *Journal of Contemporary Law* 6: 161–176.

Handberg, Roger, and Harold F. Hill Jr. 1980. Court Curbing, Court Reversals, and Judicial Review: The Supreme Court versus Congress. *Law & Society Review* 14(2): 309–322.

Hansford, Thomas, and James F. Spriggs II. 2006. *The Politics of Precedent.* Princeton: Princeton University Press.

Harrison, John. 2000. The Power of Congress over the Rules of Precedent. *Duke Law Journal* 50(2): 503–544.

Hart, Henry M., Jr. 1959. Foreword: The Time Chart of the Justices. *Harvard Law Review* 73: 84–125.

Hartnett, Edward A. 2005. The Court Clears Its Throat. *Constitutional Commentary* 22(3): 553–584.

Harvey, Anna. 2008. What Makes a Judgment Liberal? Coding Bias in the United States Supreme Court Database. Social Science Research Network. http:/ssrn.com/abstract=1120970.

Harvey, Anna, and Barry Friedman. 2006. Pulling Punches: Congressional Constraints on the Supreme Court's Constitutional Rulings, 1987–2000. *Legislative Studies Quarterly* 31: 533–562.

Hayo, Bernd, and Stephen Voigt. 2007. Explaining Defacto Judicial Independence. *International Review of Law and Economics* 27(3): 269–290.

Hedge, David, and Renee J. Johnson. 2002. The Plot That Failed: The Republican Revolution and Congressional Control of the Bureaucracy. *Journal of Public Administration Research and Theory* 12: 333–351.

Hellman, Arthur. 1985. Case Selection in the Burger Court: A Preliminary Inquiry. *Notre Dame Law Review* 60: 947–1049.

Hellman, Arthur. 1996. The Shrunken Docket of the Rehnquist Court. *Supreme Court Review* 1996: 403–438.

Hirschl, Ran. 2004. Towards Juristocracy: *The Origins and Consequences of the New Constitutionalism*. Cambridge: Harvard University Press.

Hoekstra, Valerie. 2005. Competing Constraints: State Court Responses to Supreme Court Decisions and Legislation on Wages and Hours. *Political Research Quarterly* 58: 317–328.

Hoffman, David. 1998. Bush Draws Contrasts with Rival. *Washington Post*, November 2.

Holmes, Oliver Wendell. 1920. *Collected Legal Papers*. New York: Harcourt Brace.

Howard, Robert M., and Jeffrey A. Segal. 2004. A Preference for Deference? The Supreme Court and Judicial Review. *Political Research Quarterly* 57: 131–143.

Humphries, Martha A., and Donald R. Songer. 1999. Law and Politics in Judicial Oversight of Federal Administrative Agencies. *The Journal of Politics* 61(1): 207–220.

Hutchinson, Dennis J. 1998. *The Man Who Once Was Whizzer White: A Portrait of Justice Byron R. White*. New York: Free Press.

Ignagni, Joseph, and James Meernik. 1994. Explaining Congressional Attempts to Reverse Supreme Court Decisions. *Political Research Quarterly* 47: 353–371.

Jackson, Robert H. 1955. *The Supreme Court in the American System of Government*. Cambridge: Harvard University Press.

Jackson, Vicki. 1998. Introduction: Congressional Control of Jurisdiction and the Future of the Federal Courts—Opposition, Agreement, and Hierarchy. *Georgetown Law Journal* 86(7): 2445–2480.

Jones, Bryan. 1994. *Reconceiving Decision Making in Democratic Politics*. Chicago: University of Chicago Press.

Jones, Jeffrey M. 2008. Gallop Polls: Trust in Government Remains Low. Available at http://www.gallup.com/poll/110458/Trust-Government-Remains-Low.aspx (accessed December 29, 2008).

Justice, William Wayne. 1997. The Two Faces of Judicial Activism. In *Judges on Judging: Views from the Bench*, ed. David M. O'Brien, 302-314.Washington, D.C.: Congressional Quarterly, Inc.

Kahle, Lisa M. 2005. Comment: Making "Lemon-Aid" from the Supreme Court's Lemon: Why Current Establishment Clause Jurisprudence Should Be Replaced by a Modified Coercion Test. *San Diego Law Review* 42(1): 349–404.

Kalman, Laura. 1996. *The Strange Career of Legal Liberalism*. New Haven: Yale University Press.

Keck, Thomas M. 2004. *The Most Activist Supreme Court in History*. Chicago: University of Chicago Press.

Kerr, Orin S. 2003. Upholding the Law. *Legal Affairs* (March/April): 31–34.

Klein, David E. 2008. Modesty, of a Sort, in the Setting of Precedents. *North Carolina Law Review* 86: 1213–1250.

Kmiec, Keenan D. 2004. The Origin and Current Meaning of "Judicial Activism." *California Law Review* 92(5): 1441–1478.

Komesar, Neal K. 2001. Law's Limits: *Rule of Law and the Supply and Demand of Rights*. Cambridge: Cambridge University Press.

Kozlowski, Mark. 2003. *The Myth of the Imperial Judiciary: Why the Right is Wrong about the Courts*. New York: New York University Press.

Kramer, Elsa F. 2007. Ginsburg Discusses Women's History, Legal Education. *Res Gestae*, April.

Krehbiel, Keith. 1998. *Pivotal Politics: A Theory of U.S. Lawmaking*. Chicago: University of Chicago Press.

Kristof, Nicholas D. 2005. Order in the Court. *New York Times*, October 4.

Kurland, Philip B. 1970. *Politics, the Constitution, and the Warren Court*. Chicago: University of Chicago Press.

Lamb, Charles M. 1984. Judicial Restraint on the Supreme Court. In *Supreme Court Activism and Restraint*, ed. Stephen C. Halpern and Charles M. Lamb, 7-36. Lexington, MA: Lexington Books.

Lane, Charles. 2005. Conservative's Book on Supreme Court is a Best Seller. *Washington Post*, March 20.

Langfred, Christine. 1994. The Judicialization of Politics in Germany. *International Political Science Review* 15(2): 113–124.

Larkins, Christopher M. 1996. Judicial Independence and Democratization: A Theoretical and Conceptual Analysis. *The American Journal of Comparative Law* 44(4): 605–626.

Lazarus, Edward. 1999. *Closed Chambers: The Rise, Fall, and Future of the Modern Supreme Court*. New York: Penguin Group.

Levin, Mark R. 2005. *Men in Black: How the Supreme Court is Destroying America*. Washington, D.C.: Regnery Publishing, Inc.

Levinson, Sanford. 1973. The Democratic Faith of Felix Frankfurter. *Stanford Law Review* 25: 430–48.

Levy, Robert A. and William Mellor. 2008. *The Dirty Dozen: How Twelve Supreme Court Cases Radically Expanded Government and Eroded Freedom*. New York: Sentinel.

Levy, Richard E., and Robert L. Glicksman. 1989. Judicial Activism and Restraint in the Supreme Court's Environmental Law Decisions. *Vanderbilt Law Review* 42(2): 343–432.

Lewis, Anthony. 1987. Abroad at Home: "Up to the Judges." *New York Times*, August 13.

Lewis, Frederick P. 1999. *The Context of Judicial Activism: The Endurance of the Warren Court Legacy in a Conservative Age*. Lanham, MD: Rowman & Littlefield Publishers.

Lewis, Neil A. 2003. Conservatives Furious Over Court's Direction. *New York Times*, June 27.

Lincoln, Abraham. 1861. First Inaugural Address. Available at http://www.national-center.org/LincolnFirstInaugural.html (accessed December 29, 2008).

Lindquist, Stefanie A., Joseph L. Smith, and Frank B. Cross. 2007. The Rhetoric of Restraint and the Ideology of Activism. *Constitutional Commentary* 24(1): 103–125.

Lindquist, Stefanie A., and Rorie Spill Solberg. 2007. Judicial Review by the Burger and Rehnquist Courts. *Political Research Quarterly* 60(1): 71–90.

Maltzman, Forrest, James F. Spriggs II, and Paul J. Wahlbeck. 1999. Strategy and Judicial Choice: New Institutionalist Approaches to Supreme Court Decision-Making. In *Supreme Court Decision-Making: New Institutionalist Approaches*, ed.

Cornell W. Clayton and Howard Gillman, 43-64. Chicago: University of Chicago Press.

Marshall, Thomas R. 1989. *Public Opinion and the Supreme Court.* New York: Routledge.

Marshall, William P. 2002. Conservatives and the Seven Sins of Judicial Activism. *University of Colorado Law Review* 73(4): 1217–1256.

McCubbins, Matthew D., and Thomas Schwartz. 1984. Congressional Oversight Overlooked: Police Patrols versus Fire Alarms. *American Journal of Political Science* 28(1): 165–179.

McCubbins, Matthew D., Roger G. Noll, and Barry R. Weingast. 1987. Administrative Procedures as Instruments of Political Control. *Journal of Law, Economics, and Organization* 3: 243–277.

Meernik, James, and Joseph Ignagni. 1997. Judicial Review and Coordinate Construction of the Constitution. *American Journal of Political Science* 41: 447–467.

Meier, Kenneth J., Robert D. Wrinkle, and J.P. Polinard. 1999. Representative Democracy and Distributional Equity: Addressing the Hard Question. *Journal of Politics* 61(4): 1025–1039.

Merrill, Thomas W. 2003. The Making of the Second Rehnquist Court: A Preliminary Analysis. *St. Louis University Law Journal* 47: 569–657.

Merrill, Thomas W. 2005. Originalism, Stare Decisis and the Promotion of Judicial Restraint. *Constitutional Commentary* 22(2): 271–288.

Miles, Thomas J., and Cass R. Sunstein. 2006. Do Judges Make Regulatory Policy? An Empirical Investigation of "Chevron." *University of Chicago Law Review* 73(3): 823–882.

Miles, Thomas J., and Cass R. Sunstein. 2007. Verdict on the Supremes. *Los Angeles Times*, October 23.

Miles, Thomas J., and Cass R. Sunstein. 2007a. Response to Whalen. Available at http://volokh.com/archives/archive_2007_10_28-2007_11_03.shtml#1193935625 (accessed on October 27, 2008).

Miller, Arthur Selwyn. 1982. *Toward Increased Judicial Activism.* Westport, CT: Greenwood Publishing Group.

Miller, Arthur Selwyn. 1984. In Defense of Judicial Activism. In *Supreme Court Activism and Restraint*, ed. Stephen C. Halpern and Charles M. Lamb, 167-200. Lexington, MA: Lexington Books.

Miller, Mark. 1997. Men in Black. *Wall Street Journal*, April 24.

Mishler, William, and Reginald S. Sheehan. 1993. The Supreme Court as a Countermajoritarian Institution? The Impact of Public Opinion on Supreme Court Decisions. *The American Political Science Review* 87(1): 87–101.

Moe, Terry M. 1985. Control and Feedback in Economic Regulation: The Case of the NLRB. *American Political Science Review* 79: 1094–1116.

Nagel, Stuart. 1965. Court-Curbing Periods in American History. *Vanderbilt Law Review* 18(3): 925–944.

Neil, Martha. 2005. Half of U.S. Sees "Judicial Activism Crisis." American Bar Association. Available at http://www.abanet.org/journal/ereport/s30survey.html (accessed June 2008).

Nelson, William E. 2003. Justice Byron R. White: His Legacy for the Twenty-First Century. *University of Colorado Law Review* 74(4): 1291–1304.

New York Times. 1988. Judicial Activism, Reagan-Style. Editorial, June 29.

New York Times. 1999. Supreme Mischief. Editorial, June 24.

O'Brien, David M. 2005. A Diminished Plenary Docket. *Judicature* 89: 134–137.

O'Scannlain, Diarmuid F. 2004. On Judicial Activism. *Open Spaces Quarterly* 3(1). http://www.open-spaces.com/article-v3n1-oscannlain.php.

Paulsen, Michael Stokes. 2003. The Worst Constitutional Decision of All Time. *Notre Dame Law Review* 78(4): 995–1044.

Peabody, Bruce G. 2007. Legislating from the Bench: A Definition and a Defense. *Lewis and Clark Law Review* 11: 185–232.

Peretti, Terri Jennings. 1999. *In Defense of a Political Court*. Princeton: Princeton University Press.

Peters, Christopher. 1997. Adjudication as Representation. *Columbia Law Review* 97(2): 312–436.

Pierce, Richard. J. 1999. Is Standing Law or Politics? *North Carolina Law Review* 77(5): 1741–1790.

Pierce, Richard J., Sidney A. Shapiro, and Paul R. Verkuil. 2004. *Administrative Law and Process*. 4th ed. St. Paul, MN: Foundation Press.

Posner, Richard A. 1991. Democracy and Distrust Revisited. *Virginia Law Review* 77: 641–651.

Posner, Richard A. 1996. *The Federal Courts: Challenge and Reform*. Cambridge: Harvard University Press.

Posner, Richard A. 1998. Against Constitutional Theory. *New York University Law Review* 73: 1–22.

Posner, Richard A. 2005. Foreword: A Political Court. *Harvard Law Review* 119(1): 32–102.

Posner, Richard A. 2008. In Defense of Looseness. *The New Republic*, August 27.

Posner, Richard A. 2008a. *How Judges Think*. Cambridge: Harvard University Press.

Powe, Lucas A., Jr. 2000. *The Warren Court and American Politics*. Cambridge: Harvard University Press.

Powell, Lewis F., Jr., Rhesa H. Barksdale, David M. Ebel, Lance Liebman, and Charles Fried. 1993. A Tribute to Byron R. White. *Harvard Law Review* 107(1): 1–29.

Powers, Stephen P., and Stanley Rothman. 2002. *The Least Dangerous Branch? Consequences of Judicial Activism*. Westport: Praeger Publishers.

Prillaman, William C. 2000. *The Judiciary and Democratic Decay in Latin America*. Westport: Praeger Publishers.

Rabkin, Jeremy. 1989. *Judicial Compulsions*. New York: Basic Books.

Rathjen, Gregory J., and Harold J. Spaeth. 1979. Access to the Federal Courts: An Analysis of Burger Court Policy Making. *American Journal of Political Science* 23(2): 360–382.

Rathjen, Gregory J., and Harold J. Spaeth. 1983. Denial of Access and Ideological Preferences: An Analysis of the Voting Behavior of the Burger Court Justices, 1969–1976. *The Western Political Quarterly* 36(1): 71–87.

Raymond, John Walter. 1992. *Dictionary of Politics*. Lawrenceville, NJ: Brunswick Publishing Corporation.

Reagan, Ronald. 1985. Remarks During a White House Briefing for United States Attorneys. *Weekly Compilation Of Presidential Documents* (October 21). 21: 1276.

Reagan, Ronald. 1987. The Criminal Justice Reform Act of 1987. *Weekly Compilation Of Presidential Documents* (October 16). 23: 1185.

Reske, Henry J. 1995. The Diverse Legacy of Warren Burger. *ABA Journal* 81: 36–37.

Republican Party. 1996. Republican Party Platform of 1996. Available at http://www.presidency.ucsb.edu/ws/index.php?pid=25848 (accessed December 28, 2008).

Republican Party. 2000. Republican Party Platform of 2000. Available at http://www.presidency.ucsb.edu/ws/index.php?pid=25849 (accessed December 28, 2008).

Republican Party. 2004. Republican Party Platform of 2004. Available at http://www.presidency.ucsb.edu/ws/index.php?pid=25850 (accessed December 28, 2008).

Ringhand, Lori A. 2007. Judicial Activism: An Empirical Examination of Voting Behavior on the Rehnquist Natural Court. *Constitutional Commentary* 24(1): 43–102.

Ringhand, Lori A. 2007. The Rehnquist Court: A "By the Numbers" Retrospective. *University of Pennsylvania Journal of Constitutional Law* 9(4): 1033–1081.

Ringquist, Evan. 1995. Political Control and Policy Impact in EPA's Office of Water Quality. *American Journal of Political Science* 39: 336–363.

Roach, Kent. 2001. *The Supreme Court on Trial: Judicial Activism or Democratic Dialogue*. Toronto: Irwin Law.

Roberts, Caprice L. 2007. In Search of Judicial Activism: Dangers of Quantifying the Qualitative. *Tennessee Law Review* 74(4): 567–622.

Rodriguez, Dan B. 1992. Statutory Interpretation and Political Advantage. *International Review of Law and Economics* 12(2): 217–231.

Rogers, James R., and Georg Vanberg. 2007. Resurrecting Lochner: A Defense of Unprincipled Judicial Activism. *The Journal of Law, Economics, and Organization* 23(2): 442–468.

Roosevelt, Kermit, III. 2006. *The Myth of Judicial Activism*. New Haven: Yale University Press.

Roots, Roger. 2001. Are Cops Constitutional? *Seton Hall Constitutional Law Journal* 2001: 685–755.

Rosenberg, Gerald. 1991. *The Hollow Hope: Can Courts Bring About Social Change?* Chicago: University of Chicago Press.

Rosenberg, Gerald. 1992. Judicial Independence and the Reality of Political Power. *The Review of Politics* 54(3): 369–398.

Sandefur, Timothy. 2004. The Wolves and the Sheep of Constitutional Law: A Review Essay on Kermit Roosevelt's *The Myth of Judicial Activism*. *Journal of Law and Politics* 23: 1–40.

Schauer, Frederick. 1987. Precedent. *Stanford Law Review* 39(3): 571–605.

Schick, Marvin. 1984. Judicial Activism on the Supreme Court. In *Supreme Court Activism and Restraint*, ed. Stephen C. Halpern and Charles M. Lamb, 37–56. Lexington, MA: Lexington Books.

Schlafly, Phyllis 2002. Judicial Activism: The Biggest 2002 Election Issue. *The Schlafly Report* 36(3). http://www.eagleforum.org/psr/2002/oct02/psroct02.shtml (accessed July 21, 2008).

Schlesinger, Arthur M. 1947. The Supreme Court: 1947. *Fortune*, January.

Schwartz, Bernard. 1997. *A Book of Legal Lists.* New York: Oxford University Press.

Scott, Kevin M. 2006. Shaping the Supreme Court's Certiorari Docket. *Justice System Journal* 27(2): 191–207.

Segal, Jeffrey A. 1997. Separation-of-Powers Games in the Positive Theory of Congress and Courts. *American Political Science Review, 91*(1), 28–44.

Segal, Jeffrey A., and Robert M. Howard. 2001. How the Supreme Court Justices Respond to Litigant Requests to Overturn Precedent. *Judicature* 85(3): 148–157.

Segal, Jeffrey A., and Robert M. Howard. 2002. An Original Look at Originalism. *Law & Society Review* 36(1): 113–138.

Segal, Jeffrey A., and Harold J. Spaeth. 1993. *The Supreme Court and the Attitudinal Model.* Cambridge: Cambridge University Press.

Segal, Jeffrey A., and Harold J. Spaeth. 2002. *The Supreme Court and the Attitudinal Model Revisited.* Cambridge: Cambridge University Press.

Seper, Jerry. 2004. Ashcroft Rips Federal Judges on National Security. *Washington Times*, November 13.

Shapiro, Carolyn. Forthcoming. Coding Complexity: Bringing Law to the Empirical Analysis of the Supreme Court. *Hastings Law Journal* 60.

Shapiro, Martin, and Alec Stone Sweet. 2002. *On Law, Politics and Judicialization.* New York: Oxford University Press.

Shapiro, Sidney A., and Richard E. Levy. 1995. Judicial Incentives and Indeterminacy in Substantive Review of Administrative Decisions. *Duke Law Journal* 44(6): 1051–1080.

Sheehan, Reginald S. 1992. Federal Agencies and the Supreme Court: An Analysis of Litigation Outcomes, 1953–1988. *American Politics Research* 20(4): 478–500.

Sherry, Suzanna. 2001. Too Clever by Half: The Problem with Novelty in Constitutional Law. *Northwestern University Law Review* 95(3): 921–932.

Sherry, Suzanna. 2007. Democracy and the Death of Knowledge. *University of Cincinnati Law Review* 75: 1053–1069.

Shiffman, Stuart. 1992. Review of Felix Frankfurter: *Judicial Restraint and Individual Liberties*, by Melvin Urofsky. *Judicature* 75: 278–279.

Siegel, Andrew M. 2006. The Court against the Courts: Hostility to Litigation as an Organizing Theme in the Rehnquist Court's Jurisprudence. *Texas Law Review* 84(5): 1097–1202.

Siegel, Jonathan R. 2007. A Theory of Justiciability. *Texas Law Review* 86(1): 73–139.

Silverstein, Mark, and Benjamin Ginsberg. 1987. The Supreme Court and the New Politics of Judicial Power. *Political Science Quarterly* 102(3): 371–388.

Sinclair, Michael. 2007. Precedent, Super-Precedent. *George Mason Law Review* 14: 363–411.

Smith, Joseph L. 2007. Presidents, Justices, and Deference to Administrative Action. *Journal of Law, Economics, and Organization* 23(2): 346–364.

Smith, Loren A. 1985. Judicialization: The Twilight of Administrative Law. *Duke Law Journal* 1985(2): 427–466.

Smith, Stephen F. 2002. Activism as Restraint: Lessons from Criminal Procedure. *Texas Law Review* 80(5): 1057–1116.

Solberg, Rorie Spill, and Stefanie A. Lindquist. 2006. Activism, Ideology, and Federalism: Judicial Behavior in Constitutional Challenges before the Rehnquist Court, 1986 to 2000. *Journal of Empirical Legal Studies* 3(2): 37–261.

Sowell, Thomas. 2004. When Rhetoric Beats Reasoning: The Baneful Consequences of *Brown v. Board of Education. Wall Street Journal*, May 16.

Spaeth, Harold J. 1964. The Judicial Restraint of Mr. Justice Frankfurter—Myth or Reality? *American Journal of Political Science* 8: 22–38.

Spaeth, Harold. 2005. United States Supreme Court Judicial Database, 1953-2005. Ann Arbor, MI: Inter-University Consortium for Political and Social Research. Available at http://www.cas.sc.edu/poli/juri/.

Spriggs, James F., II, and Thomas G. Hansford. 2001. Explaining the Overruling of U.S. Supreme Court Precedent. *Journal of Politics* 63(4): 1091–1111.

Stearns, Maxwell L. 2007. The Political Economy of the Roberts Court. Social Science Research Network. Available at http://papers.ssrn.com/sol3/papers.cfm?abstract_id=976693.

Stevens, John Paul. 1983. The Life Span of a Judge-Made Rule. *New York University Law Review* 58(1): 1–21.

Stone, Geoffrey R. 1988. Precedent, the Amendment Process, and Evolution in Constitutional Doctrine. *Harvard Journal of Law & Public Policy* 11(1): 67–74.

Stone Sweet, Alec. 2002. *Governing with Judges: Constitutional Politics in Europe.* New York: Oxford University Press.

Sunstein, Cass R. 1991. What's Standing after *Lujan*? Of Citizen Suits, "Injuries," and Article III. *Michigan Law Review* 91(2): 163–236.

Sunstein, Cass R. 1999. *One Case at a Time: Judicial Minimalism on the Supreme Court.* Cambridge: Harvard University Press.

Sunstein, Cass R. 2001. Tilting the Scales Rightward. *New York Times*, April 26.

Sunstein, Cass R. 2005. Radicals in Robes: *Why Extreme Right-Wing Courts Are Wrong for America.* New York: Basic Books.

Sutherland, Mark, ed. 2005. *Judicial Tyranny: The New Kings of America.* St. Louis: Amerisearch, Inc.

Taggart, William, and Matthew DeZee. 1985. A Note on Substantive Access Doctrines in the U.S. Supreme Court: A Comparative Analysis of the Warren and Burger Courts. *The Western Political Quarterly* 38(1): 84–93.

Tate, C. Neal, and Torbjorn Vallinder. 1997. *The Global Expansion of Judicial Power.* New York: New York University Press.

Thayer, James Bradley. 1893. The Origin and Scope of the American Doctrine of Constitutional Law. *Harvard Law Review* 7: 129–156.

Toma, Eugenia F. 1991. Congressional Influence and the Supreme Court: The Budget as a Signaling Device. *Journal of Legal Studies* XX: 131–146.

Tribe, Lawrence H. 1981. Jurisdictional Gerrymandering: Zoning Disfavored Rights Out of the Federal Courts. *Harvard Civil Rights-Civil Liberties Law Review* 16(1): 129–156.

Tushnet, Mark. 1998. Byron White: The Football Player as Supreme Court Justice. *Green Bag* 1(2): 419–423.

Tushnet, Mark. 1999. *Taking the Constitution Away from the Courts.* Princeton: Princeton University Press.

Urofsky, Melvin. 1991. *Felix Frankfurter; Judicial Restraint and Individual Liberties.* New York: Twayne Publishers.

U.S. House. 2004. *Congressional Record.* 108th Cong., 2d Sess. Vol. 150: 7825.

U.S. House. 2004a. *Congressional Record.* 108th Cong., 2d Sess. Vol. 150: 6580.

U.S. Senate. 1956. The Southern Manifesto. *Congressional Record.* 84th Cong., 2d Sess. Vol. 102, pt. 4: 4459–4460.

U.S. Senate. 1987. *Congressional Record.* 100th Cong., 1st Sess. Vol. 133: 14767.

U.S. Senate. 1987a. *Congressional Record.* 100th Cong., 1st Sess. Vol. 133: 14985.

U.S. Senate. 1990. Committee on the Judiciary. *Confirmation Hearing on the Nomination of David Souter to be Associate Justice of the United States.* 101st Cong., 2nd Sess. Washington, D.C.: Government Printing Office.

U.S. Senate 1997. Committee on the Judiciary. *Judicial Activism: Defining the Problem and Its Impact: Hearing before the Subcommittee on the Constitution, Civil Rights and Property Rights of the United States Senate.* 105th Cong., 1st Sess. Washington, D.C.: Government Printing Office.

U.S. Senate. 2004. Committee on the Judiciary. *Judicial Activism vs. Democracy: What Are the National Implications of the Massachusetts Goodridge Decision and the Judicial Invalidation of Traditional Marriage Laws?: Hearing before the Subcommittee on the Constitution, Civil Rights and Property Rights of the United States Senate.* 108th Cong., 2d Sess. Washington, D.C.: Government Printing Office.

U.S. Senate. 2005. *Congressional Record.* 109th Cong., 2d Sess. Vol. 151: 10395.

U.S. Senate. 2005a. *Congressional Record.* 109th Cong., 2d Sess. Vol. 151: 10481.

U.S. Senate. 2005b. Committee on the Judiciary. *Confirmation Hearing on the Nomination of John G. Roberts, Jr. to be Chief Justice of the United States.* 109th Cong., 1st Sess. Washington D.C.: Government Printing Office.

U.S. Senate. 2006. *Congressional Record.* 109th Cong., 2d Sess. Vol. 152: 334.

U.S. Senate. 2006a. *Congressional Record.* 109th Cong., 2d Sess. Vol. 152: 3507.

Vermeule, Adrian. 2005. The Judiciary Is a They, Not an It: Interpretive Theory and the Fallacy of Division. *Journal of Contemporary Legal Issues* 14(2): 549–584.

Wall Street Journal. 1997. Affirming the Voters. Editorial, April 9.

Wallace, J. Clifford. 1997. The Jurisprudence of Judicial Restraint: A Return to the Moorings. In *Judges on Judging: Views from the Bench,* ed. David M. O'Brien, 163-174. Washington, D.C.: Congressional Quarterly, Inc.

Walsh, Edward. 2000. An Activist Court Mixes Its High-Profile Messages. *Washington Post,* July 2.

Wasby, Stephen. 1976. *Continuity and Change: From the Warren to the Burger Court.* Pacific Palisades, CA: Goodyear Publishing.

Watson, George, and John Stookey. 1988. Supreme Court Confirmation Hearings: A View from the Senate. *Judicature* 71(4): 186–196.

Wechsler, Herbert. 1954. The Political Safeguards of Federalism: The Role of the States in the Composition and Selection of the National Government. *Columbia Law Review* 54(4): 543–560.

Weingast, Barry R., and Mark J. Moran. 1983. Bureaucratic Discretion or Congressional Control? Regulatory Policymaking by the Federal Trade Commission. *The Journal of Political Economy* 91(5): 765–800.

Weinreb, Lloyd L. 1982. Judicial Activism. *New York Times*, February 3.

Wells, Michael. 1994. French and American Judicial Opinions. *Yale Journal of International Law* 19(1): 81–134.

Wermiel, Stephen. 1984. The Burger Years: High Court Cuts Back Some, Overturns Few Rulings of Warren Era. *Wall Street Journal*, June 14.

Whelan, Edward. 2007. Judicial Activism Awards Fixed! *Los Angeles Times*, October 24.

Whitford, Andrew. 2002. Bureaucratic Discretion, Agency Structure, and Democratic Responsiveness: The Case of the United States Attorneys. *Journal of Public Administration Research and Theory* 12(1): 3–27.

Wicker, Tom. 2002. Foreword: Reflections of a Court Watcher. In *The Rehnquist Court*, ed. Herman Schwartz, 3–12. New York: Hill and Wang.

Wilkins, Richard G., Scott Worthington, John J. Nielsen, and Peter J. Jenkins. 2007. Supreme Court Voting Behavior 2005 Term. *Hastings Constitutional Law Quarterly* 34(4): 505–589.

Wilkinson, J. Harvie, III. 2002. Is There a Distinctive Conservative Jurisprudence? *University of Colorado Law Review* 73: 1383–1402.

Wilkinson, J. Harvie, III. 2008. *Of Guns, Abortions, and the Unraveling Rule of Law.* Social Science Research Network. Available at http://ssrn.com/abstract=1265118.

Wilson, James G. 1993. The Role of Public Opinion in Constitutional Interpretation. *Brigham Young University Law Review* 1993: 1037–1138.

Wolfe, Christopher. 1997. *Judicial Activism: Bulwark of Freedom or Precarious Security?* Lanham, MD: Rowman and Littlefield Publishers, Inc.

Wood, B. Dan, and Richard W. Waterman. 1991. The Dynamics of Political Control of the Bureaucracy. *American Political Science Review* 85(3): 801–828.

Woodward, Bob, and Scott Armstrong. 1979. *The Brethren: Inside the Supreme Court.* New York: Simon and Schuster.

Wright, J. Skelly. 1971. Professor Bickel, the Scholarly Tradition and the Supreme Court. *Harvard Law Review* 84(4): 769–805.

Yalof, David A. 1999. *Pursuit of Justices: Presidential Politics and the Selection of Supreme Court Nominees.* Chicago: University of Chicago Press.

Young, Ernest A. 2002. Judicial Activism and Conservative Politics. *University of Colorado Law Review* 73(4): 1139–1216.

Zeigler, Donald H. 1996. The New Activist Court. *American University Law Review* 45: 1367–1401.

Zietlow, Rebecca E. 2008. The Judicial Restraint of the Warren Court (and Why it Matters). *Ohio State Law Journal* 69: 255–299.

Table of Cases

Index